THE BULLSEYE™ PRINCIPLE

TARGETING YOUR BUSINESS

multi-award-winning retailer

Barry Bull

MACMILLAN

Pan Macmillan Australia

First published 2006 in Australia by Pan Macmillan Australia Pty Limited
1 Market Street, Sydney

National Library of Australia
Cataloguing-in-Publication data:

ISBN-13: 978-1-4050-3717-4
ISBN-10: 1-4050-3717-2

Bull, Barry, 1942-
The Bullseye Principle

1. Bull, Barry, 1942- . 2. Toombul Music. 3. Music stores
- Queensland - Toombul. 4. Businessmen - Queensland -
Biography. I. Title.

338.76178099431

Typeset in Palatino Linotype
Designed by Allan Cornwell
Produced by Pennon Publishing Pty Ltd
Printed by McPhersons Print Group, Maryborough, Victoria

Acknowledgements

This book came about with a little help from my friends:

Deb Haddock, Peter Marsh, Peter Kirk, Stephen Gray, Melinda Nimmo, Bev Friend, Allan Cornwell, Grant Hirst, Keith Bennett, Peter Butler, Denis Handlin AM, Peter Beattie MP and with special appreciation to my family, Kayleen, Justin, Gavin and Anissa.

Dedicated to a wonderful new generation of Little Bulls:

Alex, Sam, Connor, Jackson, Isaac

Contents

About the author

t's not every day that people get to rub shoulders with the rich and famous, but for Barry Bull, working with celebrities is normal.

Barry is a respected and highly awarded businessman in his own right. According to Richard Wilkins of 'The Today Show', he is 'an absolute legend in the Australian music industry'.

Barry Bull's career began in music retailing in 1958. After hours he would strap on his guitar and play on Brisbane's booming band circuit with his band The Counts. He was recruited by a record company, CBS Records (now Sony/BMG Entertainment), and rose through the ranks to become national marketing chief in the seventies. In 1981, after giving rock 'n' roll the best years of his life, he returned to Brisbane with the ambition to shape his own destiny. It was then that he acquired Toombul Music.

Over the years, Toombul Music has won over thirty Westfield retail awards, including winning the prestigious National Individual Specialty Retailer Award three times. In 1997 it was an inaugural inductee into the Westfield Hall of Fame in recognition of outstanding retail achievement. In 2001 Barry was presented with a Westfield Legend Award, and in 2003 was honoured with a Commonwealth Centenary Medal for distinguished achievement in business.

His innovative marketing techniques have seen Barry entice music celebrities and superstars from around the world, including Sir Cliff Richard, Michael Crawford, John Denver, Olivia Newton John, The Corrs, Ronan Keating and dozens more, to participate in promotions at his store in Brisbane.

Barry has fast become one of the country's top business speakers and 'No is Negotiable' has become his most renowned trademark. His energetic presentations share the experience of a remarkable journey, and his famous interviews with Sir Cliff Richard, Michael Crawford and Slim Dusty, wowed audiences around Australasia.

Barry has devoted a career spanning over forty years to his lifetime passion – music. At a time when most would think he would put the Bull out to pasture … he wrote a best-selling book, *A Little Bull Goes a Long Way*, followed by *My Little Book of Bull*.

Visit Barry's web site on: www.barrybull.com

Foreword

Peter Beattie MP, Premier of Queensland

Y ou've got to be smart to succeed in small business. Let's face it, you've got to be smart to succeed anywhere in this day and age!

You either innovate or you stagnate.

One of the priorities of the Smart State strategy for Queensland is to provoke all small businesses – no matter how small they are, where they are or what they sell – into thinking smart.

How can I improve the way I do business? Are there new methods I can adopt? What new technology can I employ? How can I make my product even more competitive?

Unless you're smart and are constantly asking these questions you're at risk of stagnating.

Barry Bull is a businessman who's been asking questions like these since he was in short pants.

He became national marketing chief of a record company but for the past quarter of a century he has been constantly innovating at his retail store, winning more than thirty Westfield retail awards.

This has led him to become a top business speaker and author, this being his third book.

Barry Bull is a smart businessman – and that's exactly the concept I am promoting through the Smart State strategy.

That's why as Premier of Queensland I had no hesitation in agreeing to write this foreword for Barry.

He's a smart thinker.

Yours sincerely,

Peter Beattie, MP

Premier and Minister for Trade

Foreword

Denis Handlin AM

P assion.

The story of how a former rock musician could take on some of the world's biggest retailers and win in the toughest, most competitive industry in the world, has to be a story of passion.

Thirty-five years ago when I started in the business Barry Bull took a chance and hired me. I started work in what was then The Australian Record Company (now Sony BMG). After a few days it became pretty clear to me that I didn't know as much as I thought I did. Luckily Barry took me under his wing. He became my mentor during those early years and we've been friends ever since.

Barry was National Marketing Director of CBS Records, and I had the real pleasure of working closely with him to launch top artists in Australia such as Billy Joel, Meatloaf, Neil Diamond, Boz Scaggs and Dragon. As I moved up in the company Barry and I worked together on concepts that were then new to the music industry. We pioneered many exciting initiatives and worked for what seemed like twenty hours a day and partied for what seemed like the other four hours.

They were heady, hard-working days but we both absolutely loved the industry.

But Barry had one burning ambition. He wanted to own his own music store. To a lot of his friends, leaving a job like that to start his own music business was not only madness but financial suicide. Even twenty years ago the idea that an independent retailer in a suburb of Brisbane could survive and grow seemed like a real fantasy.

Barry left CBS and bought Toombul Music. Since then that one store and that one guy have become legends in the music and retailing industry. Toombul Music has won over thirty Westfield awards, and has been inducted into the Westfield Hall of Fame.

In 2001 Barry was presented 'A Westfield Legend Award', acknowledging twenty years of superior retailing and in 2003 was awarded a Common-wealth Centenary Medal for distinguished achievement in business.

Barry is the flesh and blood example of the importance of passion. He reminds all of us that creativity, taking risks and a bit of luck, combined with an absolute passion for your product and your customers really pays off. His success comes from his ability to find extraordinary ways to attract and satisfy his customers. What other independent retailer could get Sir Cliff Richard, The Corrs, Ronan Keating, John Denver, Harry Connick Jr and Olivia Newton John to do an in-store appearance.

Barry has translated his success in retailing to an equally successful career as an author and motivational speaker. He has pioneered many music retail concepts including the establishment of the Australian Music Retailers Association.

Barry Bull has a great story to tell. Most importantly he's done what others just dream about. Barry absolutely lives by his motto 'No Is Negiotable'. Barry's outstanding business success has only been surpassed by having the success of a wonderful family.

Read this book, you'll love it.

Denis Handlin AM
Chairman and Chief Executive Officer
Sony/BMG Entertainment
Australia/New Zealand

Introduction

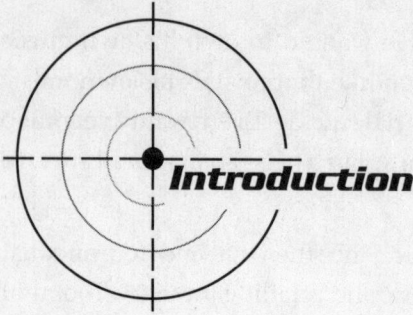

Rewind – Saturday morning some time in 1954

It was probably a balmy Brisbane morning with the sun just starting to add to the breathless humidity of a rural landscape called Indooroopilly, an outer community in Brisbane's western suburbs where I grew up. The wallabies grazed in the backyard and the melodious morning chorus of the maggies and currawongs was nature's way of heralding another perfect day.

It was an era that has long gone.

Home entertainment was the AWA radio. The Silent Knight ice box in the kitchen kept the food cool, and the Crown wood stove cooked it. The copper was Mum's washing machine. The chooks in the backyard provided the eggs for breakfast and a special treat at Christmas dinner. And the dunny was a shed in the backyard. Life was simple: no TV, fast food, washing machine, refrigerator, microwave or flushing loos in our place, and definitely no car. My constant companion, however, was an old Malvern Star bicycle. I learned many painful lessons as a result of numerous falls off my bike, while attempting to ride on the grassy slopes of nearby Moore Park. I learned that having the determination to get back on was often harder than falling off!

I was a shy twelve-year-old and was accompanying my dad on his regular weekend excursion. Every Saturday morning he would assist his local

RSL club (being a returned digger from World War II) to raise money with meat trays and chook raffles and the like. As tradition would have it, he would then spend an hour at the pub before going home for lunch. He loved nothing more than meeting his mates on Saturday. It was the social thing to do for a hard-working bloke with a young family living life in the early fifties.

There was no bar-room entertainment, no colour TVs or poker machines in those days. Just a dart board in the pub's lounge, which was always in demand by the locals who balanced a glass of 'Fourex' ale in one hand and a dart in the other. This was a game of skill that sometimes resulted in triumphant shouts of '*Bullseye*!' when someone hit the little circle in the centre. Having a name like Bull made me curious to know why my name was being shouted.

The game looked like fun, and I asked to have a go while I waited for my dad. After all, I was pretty good at hurling a cricket ball. But on my first throw, I completely missed the board and planted the dart square in the middle of the local RSL's honour board of war veterans! Not to be discouraged, I returned to the throwing line and after a few lessons from the local weekend warriors, I eventually hit the board. One of Dad's mates approached me – an old guy they called Blue, a regular at the bar. He said, 'Son, you are now in the game, and the challenge is to get as close as you can to the target in the centre. If you hit the Bullseye – you win.'

As the weeks passed I never missed an opportunity to hit that dart board. I realised this was a game of skill over which the oldies thought they had a monopoly. Eventually, with practice, I consistently hit the target. Old Blue, who had encouraged me a few weeks earlier, shuffled over and said something I always remembered:

'Son, I've been watching your progress and you've learned a valuable lesson in your determination to master the game. That dart board is like the game of life. You begin by getting on the board, and as you grow you learn from others and improve the skills that you've been given. But when you focus on doing what *you* want in your life, and are determined to get it, is when you hit your target.'

He then used an Aussie icon as an example, which is why his message was so memorable. He explained how Don Bradman, who was a huge national cricket hero, had practised and practised and fixed mistakes, until he developed superb natural skills. Through determination, he became the best cricketer in the world.

And he grinned as he said, 'With a name like *Bull* you're gifted to hit the Bullseye!' By now, I was accustomed to sarcastic jokes about my name and at the time paid no attention to his perceptive prediction.

But his mentoring came at a time when I needed inspiration. I was not doing very well at school and one teacher had written on my report card that unless I improved my marks I would never get a good job. This tactic was commonly used by some educators in those days to improve performance, but fear of failure only served to reduce whatever confidence I had. Also, having a name like Bull could make life difficult if schoolmates were unkind to under-achievers.

I looked forward to my 'lessons' from Old Blue and, paradoxically, whenever I press the replay button on my life, his words of wisdom recur time and again. As it turned out, he was right on both counts. I learned how to target ambition and my name became my best asset.

But music was soon to become my liberation.

In the early fifties radio stations mainly played music for adults: jazz, country, classical, Broadway musicals and soft ballads. The charts were dominated by pop artists such as Perry Como, Frankie Laine, Johnny Ray and Rosemary Clooney, all soft balladeers who soothed post-war adults. Teenagers were totally ignored and kids had no music that spoke to their generation. But that was about to change – a revolution was inevitable! Also I was soon to discover a phenomenon that was unlikely to ever happen again in my lifetime.

The birth of rock 'n' roll

On 5 July 1954 Sun Records in Memphis recorded a song by a shy nineteen-year-old budding superstar named Elvis Presley. That song – 'That's All Right' – would go down in history as arguably the very first rock 'n' roll single.

When I first heard Elvis it was as if a line had been drawn in the sand separating all that went before from all that followed: it was rock 'n' roll. Today we have the internet for global communication, but back in the fifties it was the radio. And it was the radio that introduced me to music. I didn't realise it at the time, but my destiny was being shaped by a music revolution called rock 'n' roll!

By 1955, Bill Haley had recorded the definitive song that galvanised rock 'n' roll in the movie *Blackboard Jungle*. 'Rock Around the Clock' would be known as the spark that ignited the birth of rock 'n' roll.

It was Elvis who ignited that spark in me and countless others of my generation. John Lennon once said, 'If there hadn't been Elvis, there wouldn't have been The Beatles.' Cliff often told me that there would have been no Cliff Richard if it hadn't been for Elvis. The establishment, however, was outraged by this intrusion into the polite world of the fifties and conservative commentators denounced this new music as a fad that would soon pass. The older generation hated Elvis and despised the influence that rock 'n' roll had on their offspring. This attitude just fuelled the revolution. The more parents protested against rock 'n' roll, the more popular it became. Teenagers were liberated from the past, rules were being broken and there was no turning back. Music encapsulated the rebellion of youth.

As time passed, my dad knew that music was more important to me than maths, so he took me for a job interview at a large music store in Brisbane called Kings (where the Myer centre in the Brisbane mall stands today). Fortunately he knew the manager and I got my first job. It was in the late fifties, I was just fifteen, and the fickle finger of fate pointed me in the right direction at the right time.

The Bee Gees were growing up in Brisbane; they were my customers. Johnny O'Keefe, Oz's first rock hero, was a regular at the shop when he was performing at Brisbane's Festival Hall. Kings was also the target for all local and international musicians. I was right in the middle of the action. I had hit the Bullseye without realising it.

Then came the sixties, and all hell broke loose. The Beatles were blazing, the Stones were getting their 'kicks on Route 66', The Beach Boys were having 'good vibrations', and Elvis was king. So, I acquired a guitar and formed my own rock 'n' roll band. Looking back, the sixties was the most exciting decade of my life.

But it was the guitar that changed everything and for the next decade it became my constant companion.

When I heard the sounds that the electric guitar was making, I wanted to be part of the revolution. The US had Elvis, the UK had Cliff and Oz had JO'K and I was hooked on the rebellious rhythm of the big beat. My parents, however, hated rock 'n' roll and suggested that if I must play music that I learn the piano accordion, which was a popular instrument at the time.

There were no guitar teachers for rock 'n' roll music, just Hawaiian clubs. Can you imagine how revolting that was to me; the thought of playing a piano accordion or a Hawaiian guitar? However, my dad became ill and lost his job, and my small wage went to help support the family, so I had no money to buy the 'cool' music box that my idols had around their necks.

In everyone's life there is someone who goes without to help you and in my case it was my grandmum. She paid five pounds for my guitar, because she knew how much I wanted to play. But without a teacher I struggled. After all, I had been told at school that I was an under-achiever and I definitely lacked the confidence to succeed. I would sit up all night practising, with sore fingers, listening to early recordings of Elvis, Cliff, Roy, and Buddy, trying to figure out how they did it.

Then one day, an old jazz musician helped me with a few basics chords and told me to practise and practise. I then recalled what Old Blue had said about Don Bradman not giving up until he achieved his dream. I had this song I wanted to play. I kept at it. Finally the key of C magically formed a harmonic sequence.

I not only became a proficient player, but eventually was able to assist others. I started my own guitar classes at Kings, when I was able to get away from my retail duties during the day and a busy band schedule at night. It didn't occur to me at the time, but I was beginning to march to the beat of my own drum.

'Business – it's only rock 'n' roll' became my anthem!

Strangely, learning to play the guitar gave me confidence that I never knew existed. I was up on stage doing something that my peers couldn't. Even those smart kids at school who'd bullied me now wanted to be mates.

One band that had a profound influence was Cliff Richard's backing group The Shadows. The sound that Hank Marvin coached from his Fender guitar was revolutionary. I had never heard anything like it and I had to have one. So, in 1962, I imported one of the first Fender guitars to Queensland. It cost a small fortune but it was the best and at this time in my young life I was ambitious to be the best. I still have this vintage icon. It is my only tangible link to a decade that transformed my youth. That guitar is probably worth more today than all the money I made as a struggling sixties rocker.

It was during this time that I met my lifelong partner and soulmate, Kayleen. Her support through the years inspired me to follow my dreams and our family success is due to her outstanding qualities.

As the end of the sixties approached I was discovered and signed to a record company. It wasn't a recording contract, but an employment contract to work for one of the biggest record companies on the planet: CBS Records (now Sony/BMG Entertainment).

Within a few short years Kayleen and I and our two young sons, Justin and Gavin, were transferred to Sydney and I was about to be catapulted from a parochial local music scene into the international arena of sex, drugs and rock 'n' roll. It wasn't long before I was promoted to marketing director of CBS Australia. This was a job that took me around the world and brought me face to face with global superstars.

A lot of people don't realise that in 1974, one in four Oz households owned a copy of Neil Diamond's *Hot August Night* and Australia was Neil's biggest territory outside the US. Also the international careers of Air Supply, Men at Work, Boz Scaggs, Meatloaf and Billy Joel all began in Australia with my team.

Although it may have seemed like I had it made, adversity clouded my life because I was never home. There was always a light on in the window when I got home but the kids were always asleep. I wasn't balancing my business values with my family values very well and I started to realise that if I could do it for CBS I could do it for myself. So in 1981 I resigned from CBS and bought an established music store in Brisbane's north side, called Toombul Music. The synchronicity of being in the right place at the right time to aquire this business from the Cleghorn family not only allowed me to change but provided an opportunity to reconnect all the values that were important to me.

I didn't have much money but I had knowledge, and knowledge is power. I had learned a lot about the music biz and a lot about myself. I was eager to capitalise on my experience and passion. It was a time that required personal courage, and self-awareness.

I had discovered that anything is achievable if you *pursue your passion*.

That means you've got to want to do it *real bad*. And *love* doing it.

Over time, I discovered by concentrating on developing my strengths rather than improving weaknesses (mostly things I wasn't interested in), I became *good* at what I liked, because I *liked* doing it. By focussing on improvement I could then become *better* and eventually be the *best*.

It's remarkable how many times in my life this mantra – *Be good, be better, be the best,* has assisted me through difficult times.

To get where you want to go you need to decide what it is you want. Then develop a strategy to get it, by setting realistic goals, stretching limits, learning from mistakes, solving problems, never losing sight of your target, and having the discipline to hit it. Aiming to *be good, be better, be the best.*

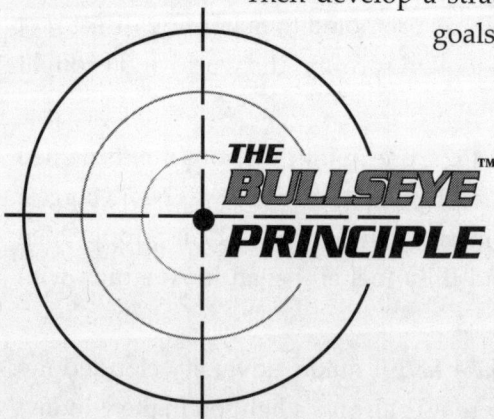

THE BULLSEYE™ PRINCIPLE

This is my Bullseye Principle.

Always have a target to aim for and a strategy to hit it.

My target with this book is to provide a *good* read and to provide *better* content and value as you work through the text. And to save the *best* for last. Now don't go flicking to the final pages because that's not what I mean. Reading a book is like life: you need to travel the full journey to gather life's experiences along the way. Slowly the entire process falls into place as knowledge combines with experience. It's the sum of all the parts, and it's called the *Book of Life*. This gives the *best* results in the most important years of our life.

Everyone needs a goal of some kind, a worthwhile belief to go forward with, and to build on. If you don't have a clear vision of where you want to go and how you're going to get there the chances are you will go nowhere. To avoid procrastination you need a destination, because procrastination prevents progress.

When I wrote my first book, *A Little Bull Goes a Long Way*, with my good mate, Ritchie Yorke, I introduced my *Hit List*. These top ten business hits were the mistakes I'd made and how I fixed them. They were the problems I'd confronted before I solved them. Not surprisingly, they became opportunities to achieve goals. Each one became a destination. Over time they all became my biggest hits, not just in my business – but in my life. You can often learn much more from mistakes than from success.

The decision to chronicle my life's work in a book assisted me to understand what I was really thinking and this exposed something that had not been apparent. I had always followed a set of procedures that were shaped and fine-tuned by the highs and lows of the journey and whose values were always somehow connected to each other. Slowly but surely, this seven-step procedure became the formula to obtain my goals. I called it the *Bullseye Principle*.

Oddly enough, Old Blue was right on target about my name. *A Little Bull Goes a Long Way* was a success and helped launch my speaking career.

I have devoted a lifetime to the music industry because, from a very young age, I've always had a song in me. The chorus to this song has been to share my passion with others. When you are doing what makes you feel good, your energy is boundless and you live your life's purpose. Of course, this was easier for me because I owned my own business.

I hope some of my enthusiasm will come across in this book. Its purpose is to assist you whether you are an independent or specialty business owner or manager. I also hope you are encouraged to find your own pathway, and to put your own individual stamp on every endeavour, to become the best at whatever it is you choose to achieve.

I share my ideas and experiences on the understanding that all of this may not necessarily be right for you, even though it was right for me. I make no apologies for focussing my story on our music retail business because that's what I do. But real commonsense stuff is applicable to any occupation or passion. And *my* songs can be sung in any key. I assure you there is nothing difficult in what I do. The difficulty is accepting that there is no substitute for effort, and that hard work only guarantees more successes than failures. Failure teaches us that persistence eventually transfers into results. I care about results. What you will read about are results that have been road tested under the most severe conditions – life in the fast lane. And it's all possible.

What will be the biggest road block to your success? It will be the difficulty that most of us have in making permanent changes in our lives to accommodate the changing times in which we live.

These days I speak at numerous conferences each year and meet some wonderful people. Being in this fortunate position has allowed me to gain valuable feedback from audiences and readers about my business attitudes. Just as importantly, I listen to their concerns and issues within their own business and family networks. Hopefully my *Bullseye Principle* will assist in solving many common problems.

The opportunity to share my experiences is an indulgence, and it allows me to put out some of what I have received. I have found that what you put out comes back to you in some way and at some time.

The chapters in this book are organised around *Barry's Bullisms*, first introduced in *My Little Book of Bull*, which brought some fun into my business life. My *Bullisms* are a collection of my favourite inspirational quotes, which have served me well over my long-playing career. They became central to my business beliefs and philosophies.

In each chapter the *Bullism* underpins these philosophies with strategies, techniques and solutions that will assist others in their search for the oxygen needed to inflate their own brands in order to remain relevant within the harsh reality of economic globalisation.

The Bullseye Principle is the sum of all of the parts of my *Bullisms*.

This book is about my experiences and the insights that I have gained while building our family enterprise. I have had valuable exposure to today's business climate through my speaking presentations to like-minded business folk throughout Australasia. It is apparent that there is a desperate need to reduce the expanding gap between the 'haves' and 'have-nots' as well as assist smaller businesses to aspire to change, establish their market niche and to coexist with the corporate culture of big business.

So many deserve success but can't seem to find it. They lose their way. That's because the road to success is always under construction.

My *Bullisms* can be the road map you need to stay on track, to avoid the road blocks of uncertainty that hinder the health and wealth of business, and to signpost the direction you need to take.

So … I'd like to share with you *The Bullseye Principle:* a simple road-tested strategy of remaining focussed on where it is you want to go and the disciplines required to get there.

And I hope you enjoy some 'good old rock 'n' roll' along the way!

Fast forward – Monday evening 5 July 2004

I am in the studio broadcasting my live weekly radio segment on Brisbane talk-back radio 4BC with host Tony Johnston. Each week I review new music releases and, as Tony refers to me as *The Music Man*, I understandably get lots of callers.

Tonight's a big night. It's the official fiftieth anniversary of rock 'n' roll.

BARRY BULL

Elvis's long-time record company BMG is celebrating the occasion with a new digitally remastered release of the song that started it all. As I played Elvis's 'That's All Right', a feeling of déjà vu came over me. My hands were shaking and my knees were weak. I was 'all shook up'. It was fifty years ago that I first heard this sound and it was just as powerful and fresh as it had been when its rebellious rhythm first touched my young life.

Memories of the fifties came flooding back. As I told this story to a live radio audience I received a call from a listener who said, 'Barry it seems you gave rock 'n' roll the best years of your life!'

My choked reply was, 'And I wouldn't have missed it for a minute!'

Barry Bull

THE BULLSEYE PRINCIPLE™

1 SET YOUR SIGHTS

**WHAT YOU WANT –
WHERE YOU WANT TO BE**

Chapter 1

Focussing your energy

BULLISM:™ VIS-A-BULL

Let the BULLDUST settle before you proceed.

Barry Bull

Winston Churchill once said: 'This is not the end, it is not even the beginning of the end, but it is the end of the beginning.' I would like to begin at the end of my first literary outing ...

In my first book, *A Little Bull Goes a Long Way*, I ended by saying that time and life wait for no one. The chances to grow and to build our life come one day at a time and have to be grasped when they arrive. To build the life you want and to increase the effectiveness of your business you need to set a plan to achieve your goals.

To achieve your dreams you need to spend your energy on what is *possible*, not on what is impossible, and in doing so, focus that energy on what you do well, what is real to you and what makes you feel good. Your ambitions don't have to match the achievements of others – everyone is different. You can be who you are and still get to the same place.

To begin a project you need to understand the game. To get runs on the scoreboard you practise, rehearse, hone skills and persist against resistance, until you finally hit the Bullseye. Once you hit your target it is easier the next time. It becomes easier if you enjoy the task because it's much easier to improve something you enjoy doing. Always give it your best shot and have your heart in it all the way.

Do what it takes to make your heart sing.
Don't die with your song still in you.

Benjamin Disraeli

Your target is *your* dream – no one else's – and the scoreboard is your scoreboard: cheat and the only person you are fooling is yourself. We all need objectives: a target to hit, a goal to achieve, no matter how big or small. I discovered that by keeping score I could measure performance and improve results until eventually I achieved dreams and goals that were unimaginable when I was struggling to gain self-confidence. It was just as important to pursue objectives that were real to me and within my physical and financial capacity. This is why I only have one store. I never wanted to be the biggest – just the best. It's the science of the possible. But don't concentrate on the possible to the exclusion of your dreams. Now is the time to '*do what it takes to make your heart sing*'. Now is the time to … *set your sights.*

Being prepared to change and adapt our life and our work to the constantly changing workplace is critical. Recognise opportunity even when it is least apparent. Challenge adversity before it becomes overwhelming; and decide that the life you have offers you the only chance in this world to become what you want to be. You can achieve everything that is wonderful, exciting and fulfilling if you are willing to dream a dream and to follow your dream. Turn it into a goal and pursue that goal with every talent you possess.

Goals are really a mechanism for turning dreams into reality. The playing field has boundaries that contain the rules and conditions to succeed within the framework of competition, good ethics and a realistic time frame. If you constantly monitor your performance you will be able to develop talent into real ability and the pursuit of your passion will become an enjoyable reality.

I was never good at numbers so I employed an accountant to support my weakness while I concentrated on my strengths: marketing and my passion for music. I have always loved rock 'n' roll so I became *good* at music marketing and as I got *better*, my goal was to be the *best*.

When I first acquired my business I went like *a Bull at a gate*, eager to succeed. I had just left a high-powered marketing job with one of the biggest record companies on the planet and this Little Bull was ready to charge. I didn't have much money after I bought our business, but I wasn't poor, I was rich in knowledge. Money without knowledge is useless. Knowledge without money is a better place to start.

Over time this knowledge developed into a successful seven-step procedure to attain my goals. It's called *The Bullseye Principle*. Here's how it works.

1. **Set your sights** – decide what you want, and where you want to be.

2. **Plan the process** – how are you going to get there, and how long it will take?

3. **Implement the strategy** – tactics, techniques and fundamentals.

4. **Deal with the issues** – solve problems, seize opportunities.

5. **Measure performance** – be good, be better, be the best.

6. **Discipline and determination** – be committed; stay focussed.

7. **Hit the Bullseye** – reap the rewards.

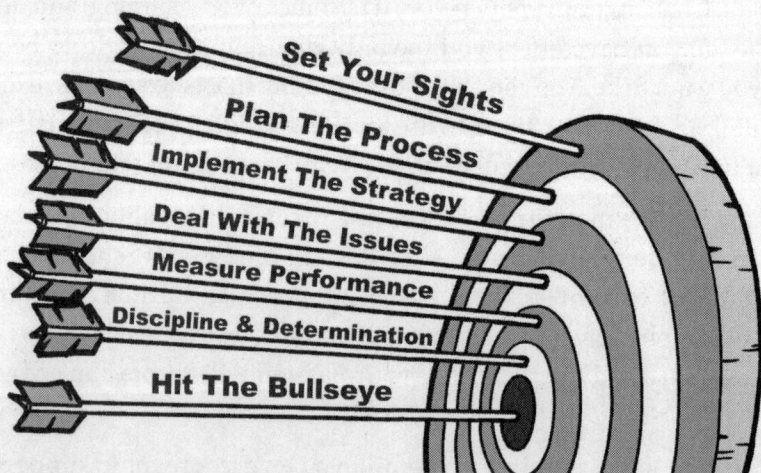

As the target illustrates, each step gets you closer to the Bullseye. That's because all seven steps are connected to each other.

I focus on my target, learn the skills and adopt the strategy that will help me to achieve my goals. Then I hit my target. There will be times when I fall: that's life. We all get knocked down. That's how we grow, learn how to progress and move forward, just as I did when I was a small boy learning to ride my bike. The pain of falling off was offset by the gains of getting back on and learning from my mistakes.

John Lennon once wrote: 'Life is what happens when we're busy making other plans.' He made a good point. So pick yourself up, learn from your mistakes, resolve problems and get back in the game. Importantly, use the experience of losing – to win. Capitalise on the frustration that disappointment brings – to eventually succeed. Once you hit the *Bullseye* you will discover as I have that *winners are recognised, rewarded and remembered.*

It's difficult, however, to succeed in business without vision. After all, what you see is what you get. I have always defined vision as seeing something others don't, looking through a window of wisdom that exposes new directions. It's my dream of opportunity; what it is I want and where I want to be.

What is your vision? Where are you now? Where do you want to be in the next five years? What is your plan to get there? What is your strategy to achieve this? You might like to consider using *The Bullseye Principle*.

Its philosophy does not just apply in business. I find that it works for most things in life. All you need is a goal to aim for and a target to hit. And a belief system that supports 'having a go' and not giving up.

Now I will explain each of the seven steps of *The Bullseye Principle*.

1. Set your sights

I can see clearly now the rain has gone, I can see all obstacles in my way.

Johnny Nash

'I can see clearly now' was a huge reggae hit back in 1972 for Johnny Nash. Whenever I hear this motivational lyric it's a powerful reminder that this is the first step in deciding what it is I want and where I want to be. It's not difficult to find your own level of success. You just need to recognise opportunities, maintain a positive attitude that this will be right for you, set your sights on the target – and have a go.

What is your dream for the future? Where do you want to be five or ten years from now – or even sooner? It's amazing how so many people live life day to day with the thought that tomorrow will always be like today. They live for now believing that tomorrow will take care of itself. Failing to plan results in planning to fail. It's often too late when we realise that we needed a plan or missed an opportunity because we lacked the courage to have a go.

Planning for the future is what we all must do, no matter what stage of our life we are at. It's never too late. It is easy, however, to lose sight of how wonderful success can be, because adversity can wear you down and distractions can become a way of life. It's so easy to adopt a reactive approach to life, constantly putting out the fires of adversity, instead of focussing on proactive ways to predict problems and prevent adversity occurring in the first place.

Let me give you an example. Surely the most valuable possession in our life is good health? Yet we spend most of our life working obsessively to attain material possessions and take our health for granted. I accept that working hard to gain wealth has always been part of life in our culture and many others; however, why is it that it's only when we receive a serious wake-up call, like the death of a loved one or an illness which threatens our quality of life, that we consider alternatives? Most degenerative diseases are preventable if we understand what we must do to maintain an active and healthy body. This is a proactive approach to preventing illness. But when illness occurs your doctor usually takes a reactive approach by prescribing medication to fix the problem. It's the same in business. Most business failures are caused by a lack of understanding of what it takes to keep a business vibrant and healthy. Most likely there was no plan and no

Most business failures are caused by a lack of understanding.

target to aim for. It was a day-to-day struggle of finding reactive remedies to survive, instead of implementing proactive procedures to improve.

Now is the time to consider your alternatives and set your sights on what it is you want to achieve in the next five years or where you want to be in the next ten – or sooner. We can be whatever we want to become and the only negatives to personal growth are those that are placed on us by ourselves. The common trait that links most successful people is they know where they are going and have a clear understanding of what they want out of life.

The Bullseye Principle sets goals, predicts problems, anticipates what it takes to succeed by implementing good strategies and committing to the achievement of the right result. It all starts here when you *set your sights* on your target. It begins when you decide what it is you want and where you want to be. Once you see the big picture you then work back from this point and plan how you are going to get there.

The moment you believe you can be anything you want to be, is the moment when your destiny is shaped.

Let me show you my target, and if you haven't yet decided on one of your own then you can share mine, because I am sure that mine contains the essentials that we all seek in our working life ... health, wealth and lifestyle.

To have the wellbeing and the financial freedom to enjoy the best years of your life is a goal everyone should aspire to and want to achieve: a dream of good health, financial security and time to do the things you want to do in your life. All you need is to see your dream in your mind, and have a method for turning imagination into reality. Imagination knows no boundaries, except for the limitations you place on your own beliefs to make your dreams come true.

If you can dream it, you can do it.

Walt Disney

2. Plan the process

Once your target is in your sights the next step is to ask how you are going to get there? How long will it take? You need to know where you're going because, if you don't, you may end up going nowhere. You need a plan.

Every structured project requires a plan. A building cannot be built without plans that show every detail of construction. Then that plan requires approvals and permits from higher authorities to ensure that the construction complies with regulations and standards so it won't fall down. It makes sense that we construct a business plan with the same fundamentals to reduce the risk of collapse and, more importantly, to achieve a strong result. Part of planning is developing strategies to determine the best path forward and how to complete the process successfully.

Knowing how to achieve goals demands determination and commitment and realising that if plan A fails there is always plan B. And if plan B fails and there is no back-up plan, you start again. Tenacity to achieve goals is the quality shared by most successful people that I know. They realise that success means hard work, commitment and determination; having a winning plan and planning to win. Most entrepreneurs seek financial freedom, and by believing they will achieve it – they usually do.

Good planning means deciding how long a project will take and setting your goals accordingly. Short-term goals are those projects that need to be achieved quickly. Medium-term goals are a pleasure because time is not of the essence and you can take longer to achieve the best result. Long-term goals are most important as they are where you want to end up and where you are likely to hit your biggest target. Long-terms goals can be career goals: you have an ambition to have the top job, be general manager, CEO, lord mayor, premier or prime minister, run your own business, whatever. Or they can be lifetime goals: having financial freedom and good health to enjoy the best years of your life.

Attaining long-term goals, however, results from successfully achieving short- and medium-term goals. For example, you need lifetime goals, but you also need annual, monthly, weekly and daily goals. Like a perfect painting; each detail contributes to the composition of the big picture. If you can see the big picture then you work back from this point and plan each detail that will be necessary to paint a masterpiece. Most people never achieve their long-term goals despite years of effort. That's why masterpieces are rare.

The reason for this in business is because there is no plan. To exist in the competitive world of commerce today every enterprise needs a written business plan. What is a business plan? To many, it's the document a financier asks for when you apply for a start-up business loan. A good business plan, however, not only builds a stronger foundation for your business it also helps clarify the real purpose of the endeavour and the financial implications that will have an impact along the way. It will predict future scenarios and allow them to be addressed before circumstances threaten progress and will set performance targets and objectives that can be measured and monitored. Planning for growth is the objective. Where are you now and where do you want to be? What will it cost to execute an idea or market a product and what return will be generated? Will the market respond and will the initiative be profitable? None of these questions can be answered without a well-prepared business plan. This is the reason for the large proportion of small business failure.

Fact file: One in five businesses fail in the first three years.

Most important of all, realise that planning is knowing what to do next.

3. Implement the strategy

Once the plan is developed the next step is to implement a strategy of tactics, techniques and fundamentals to achieve the goal. This is an important step in achieving goals because it deals with ways of building the business plan into a solid workable business model. This differentiates you from your competition and helps make your business unique, which sets it apart from others. Tactics and techniques become fundamental to developing a strategy that is yours to own and is difficult to copy. This attracts customers and allows them to judge your goods and services on something other than just price. Good strategies require creative thinking, always searching for alternatives and being prepared to modify a *good* plan with a *better* strategy to achieve the *best* result.

4. Deal with the issues

Anticipating problems and accepting responsibility for them is a good way to deal with obstacles and adversity. No matter what business we are in there will always be problems. Unresolved problems don't go away – they are road blocks to achievement and can end in disaster. Once the issues are considered and appropriate action has been taken then the gateway to opportunity opens. Some problems then become opportunities in disguise.

Where are you now?

Is your plan on track to achieve your goal?

If not what stands in your way?

What are you going to do about it?

Neglect problems and expect a Bull in a china shop. Solve problems – achieve goals.

5. Measure performance

If you measure progress on a daily basis, then small steps up the improvement ladder are easy. We all should have an annual business plan. However, the successful achievement of the annual plan depends on the effort you give to the achievement of your daily plan. Life is measured in days not years. If you give a little more each day, each week, each month, then the compounding effect of effort will make a huge impact on your annual performance.

It's what you do after you do what you're supposed to do that matters most.

That little extra effort each day is what matters the most. Particularly if you inspire your entire team to adopt the same code of conduct.

Be *good* at what you do. Measure your performance to become *better*, then set your sights on being the *best*. What you can't measure you can't improve.

There is no better example of this than the music industry. Its total performance is measured every week by sales. The industry has a performance measurement system where retailers report their weekly sales to ARIA (Australian Record Industry Association) to be compiled into a bestseller report called The Charts. Everyone in the supply chain, artists, managers, writers, producers, publishers, record companies, retailers and radio stations are influenced by the performance of the bestsellers. There is possibly no other industry whose performance is so accurately measured than the music business. All creative practitioners want to achieve number one status. Having spent a lifetime in an industry that is so publicly focussed on performance, I have always understood the spirit of competition and the value in hitting the Bullseye.

6. Be disciplined and determined

Winston Churchill once said that: 'Kites fly highest against the wind – not with it.' I found that the times I made the most progress in my life were times when I was faced with opposition and adversity. These were times when I was forced to change or face defeat. By staying focussed and committed, and never losing sight of my goals, I found ways to hit the target. But it takes discipline to stay on target. To do things that we don't find easy, or that we don't necessarily like or that we fear. It's easy to become addicted to distractions and allow procrastination to weaken our commitment.

But being determined and doing what it takes to achieve what it is you want is an attitude of mind. Negative thinking usually produces negative results and in that condition of mind, most things seem to be bad. A positive outlook, however, can make negative things seem not so bad.

Fear of failure can be the biggest dream killer, and when you combine a thought with an emotion such as fear, the energy that results often produces a negative outcome. Equally, when you combine a thought with an emotion such as enthusiasm, the energy ignites and produces a positive outcome.

The more you feed enthusiasm the more you rise above limitations.

Be aware and in control of everything you think and feel, for a thought remains merely a thought until it is linked to a driving emotion. Discipline is necessary to nurture your thoughts and control fear. Having a disciplined approach to gaining knowledge is the way to overcome fear. Your own insecurity will be challenged because the more you learn the more control you will have over circumstances that create fear. The moment you find the answers to your own inhibitions is the moment you discover your true potential.

Many people give up when they are so close to achieving their goals and it takes persistence to overcome resistance. The ninety/ten rule applies here. Ninety per cent of people give up when they are ten per cent short of success. Many businesses fail when they are in sight of their goals. Ninety per cent of managers lose determination when they're ten per cent short of achievement. Don't give up when you still have something to give.

> *Nothing is over until the moment you stop trying.*
>
> Brian Dyson, CEO Coca-Cola

This is where my *No is Negotiable* tactic enabled me to succeed on so many occasions. By not accepting *No* for an answer, I was able to negotiate a negative into a positive. It took determination, and discipline, but the result far outweighed the effort. I just *take the Bull by the horns* every time I get a negative response and turn a No into a Yes. By discipline and determination I find that a short-term No can be turned into a long-term Yes.

But more about that later …

7. Hit the Bullseye

If the previous six fundamentals are achieved then you will have every chance of hitting your targets whatever they are. But this is not the end; it is only the end of the beginning! This is where the rewards kick in.

The Bullseye Principle is a procedure that takes good initiatives to rewarding conclusions.

Once goals are achieved they become the platform for other initiatives and the same procedure begins again. You set your sights on new targets. There will be times when fear and confusion cloud your vision. If you take your time to think clearly, assess the risks, review all the options and implement a worthy plan, the right path will become vis-a-bull. The seven steps of *The Bullseye Principle* became my pathway for personal growth and business success. By applying the same principles to other asset creation initiatives such as property and superannuation, over time all my efforts were rewarded. More importantly, the two assets that are the most important of all, health and happiness, are providing me with a rewarding lifestyle during the best years of my life.

Success in business is the implementation of *good* principles combined with unwavering commitment to focus on what you can do *better* than anyone else. This will give the *best* result. However, it all starts with a clear vision of what you want and where you want to be. If you can see it you can do it.

BULLET POINTS

- The moment you believe you can be anything you want to be, is the moment when your destiny is shaped.

- Use the experience of losing to win.

- Don't be addicted to distractions and allow procrastination to weaken your commitment.

- Instead of reactive remedies to survive find a proactive procedure to improve.

- Planning is knowing what to do next.

- Often problems are opportunities in disguise.

- The more you feed enthusiasm the more you rise above limitations.

- Nothing is over until the moment you stop trying.

- If you don't have a go, you'll never know.

THE
BULLSEYE PRINCIPLE™

2 PLAN THE PROCESS

HOW ARE YOU GOING TO GET THERE?
HOW LONG WILL IT TAKE?

Chapter 2
Setting your goals

BULLISM™: ACHIEV-A-BULL

Goals are dreams with deadlines.

Diane Scharf Hunt

Goals are easy to set but can be difficult to achieve. That's because the level of commitment needed to achieve what we want has to be constant; we cannot be distracted by adversity, or the endless issues that invade our daily existence. We can all set goals. The need to achieve is reflected in the way we think, in what we think and in what we believe. Setting goals drives us to act on our beliefs until they become reality.

However, it can be a long and winding road before we achieve critical objectives. Long-term goals such as financial independence require commitment and clear focus if we are to stay on target. *The Bullseye Principle* is the road map to achieving financial freedom because each step of the journey needs to be supported by certain procedures. Long-term achievement is the sum of all the parts, of all the decisions and choices that have been made along the way. Each decision we make and each direction we choose, affects the success of the next step in our journey.

*Long-range planning does not deal with future decisions but
with the future of present decisions.*

Peter Drucker, business consultant and author

It doesn't matter if we wander off track so long as we constantly update the activities we must do to stay on target and keep working toward the plan in order to accomplish our objective. To do this we need to set goals that keep us focussed on what it is we want to achieve. The objective of goal setting is to turn dreams into reality.

One of the critical elements in setting goals is to always have a realistic time frame. This allows for life to be lived along the way and accommodates the inevitable ups and downs of daily business, which can hinder growth. But dealing with day to day problems can easily put the horizon out of focus. As long as you don't lose sight of the target that's all that matters. The road to disappointment is always paved with good intentions.

Often we set ourselves targets that are unachievable because we apply unrealistic time frames. It is important to write your goals in your diary because what gets written down gets done. It is then of equal importance to decide how long the process will take. As I explained earlier, I allocate my goals into three time zones:

- short term
- medium term
- long term

Double the deadline

Once I have written down my goals I then decide into which time zone my current goal fits and then I double the expected achievement date. That's right, *double* the deadline. Life is too fast, everything is yesterday. Get out of the fast lane. Take the time to consider how you can reach your destination safely and successfully. Be realistic, take the pressure off yourself and allow enough time to hit your target. This way, undisciplined activity isn't an excuse to avoid achieving goals.

Never confuse activity with accomplishment

Activity can easily be little more than keeping busy, or it can just be the result of being disorganised. Accomplishment is when we see a result. Activity is what is needed to achieve that result: organising the right things, strategies or people and putting them in the right place at the right time to accomplish the right result. But you need discipline to achieve this.

Someone once said: 'The pain of discipline weighs ounces and the pain of regret weighs tons.' Setting goals is definitely a discipline, but like all disciplines it is easy to let lapse. It's a shame to see energy and resources used to no avail, to realise that time was wasted because somebody failed to plan.

The key word here is *organisation*. That's what management is: organising the process and providing leadership to get a result. So you need to decide what it is you want and set realistic goals. Goals are easier to attain with a realistic timetable.

The timetable

Decide on the time frame of the project and set deadlines.

Short-term goals: tasks that need to be done now.

Medium-term goals: projects that need to be achieved in the next six months to a year.

Long-term goals: the five-year plan. Where do you want to be in the next five years or beyond?

You can have multiple goals at the same time so long as you set a realistic timetable to achieve them. This allows time to deal with the issues and solve problems without losing sight of your target.

Be sure that the daily landscape doesn't put the horizon out of focus.

The secret to attaining long-term goals is not to let short-term problems hinder the real objectives. Don't lose sight of the big picture. Success doesn't come overnight. It comes over time.

Don't lose sight of the big picture.

Solve problems – achieve goals

Business stress begins with unresolved problems. Problems don't go away and are the infection that leads to business ill health. If they are effectively dealt with, however, they can help you improve your business.

Problems are a fundamental part of achieving anything. Like steps on a ladder, you must solve each problem as it arises before you climb to the top and attain your goals. Problems exist to test the strength of an endeavour, to expose weakness and flaws, to challenge the faint hearted, so the best result can be attained.

The path to success is to resolve problems as they arise. By facing the reality of a situation head-on, you can confront the facts and act on the implications. Realising this, I go looking for all potential problems in my business *every day* and I always find them, or should I say … they always find me! Predictably, if you deal with problems early they usually never amount to much. Failure to recognise and tackle business obstacles when they arise allows them to grow out of proportion and distract your attention from the big picture. The daily landscape is so prominent that the horizon slips out of focus. This is why many fail to attain their goals.

Another secret to achieving goals is never to take No for an answer, to understand that persistence always defeats resistance.

My *No is Negotiable* theory works really well here. As I've already said, ninety per cent of people give up when they are ten per cent from achieving their goals. I find many people give up on their goals when they are so close to winning. The word that stops them is No. It's amazing what a big problem that little word can be. What's also amazing is the result you can get if you don't accept it. Most problems can be solved by negotiating issues early, providing you don't accept No for an answer and don't allow yourself to be pushed around.

I hate to be pushed around, to be bullied. After all, I am a little bloke and big businesses like to bully little blokes like me. But they're wasting their time because my name is *Bull* and when someone says No to me, it's *like a red rag to a Bull!*

Bullying, however, isn't just external competition. Bullies are alive and well within many corporations. Years ago I worked for a large corporation and gained valuable experience. The reason I chose my own business is so I could control my own destiny, not get caught up with the corporate bullies who, through their own mediocrity, insecurity and petty politics, made me a victim of the system. I had a problem because my boss had an issue and I knew it was going to stop me achieving my goals. My goals were simple: I just wanted to be happy and get on with my job. I solved my problem; I resigned and I never looked back.

Now I'm not suggesting you give up your day job. I am suggesting, however, that you don't accept an answer that supports someone else's mediocrity. The way to achieve your goals is to solve problems, overcome resistance and be persistent.

Accept disappointment not defeat. Fix problems so they don't repeat.

I have won many battles in my life by discovering that *No is Negotiable* There is one little guy, however, who likes to get in the way. His name is Murphy and 'Murphy's Law' has a habit of kicking in just when the goal is in sight. I'm sure you know what I mean. You have one of those days when nothing goes right. 'Murphy', however, was well and truly present in my life recently.

I was engaged to speak at the Mount Isa business awards in Queensland's north-west. On the way to the airport I realised that I'd forgotten my mobile phone. The flight was late; I was sitting next to a guy who was a little too large for his seat; I accidentally spilt coffee over my new shirt; I was greeted at the Mount Isa airport with forty degree temperatures and one of my bags went missing.

As I had a few hours to prepare for my presentation I headed to the venue for a rehearsal and sound check. Although I had called ahead to inform the production person of my technical requirement, when I arrived I discovered that he had the wrong connection leads and couldn't get my equipment working. When he finally located the right connectors, my laptop refused to talk to the projector. I needed professional help quickly and as I reached for my phone to call my Brisbane support technician, I remembered that I'd forgotten to bring it. I was having one of those days!

Frustrated and disappointed, I asked the guy, "What's plan B?" He said, "Don't worry, this is Mount Isa, she'll be right mate!" Not exactly the answer I was looking for, particularly as I had been engaged to challenge this attitude. It was then I noticed that the venue was the Irish Club and realised this was where 'Murphy' lived! He was on the rampage that day! However I was determined he wasn't going to beat me. By dogged persistence we finally got my PowerPoint working, just in time to take the stage and speak to 400 business people who were none the wiser. Persistence always defeats resistance; right? But 'Murphy' eventually had the final say. As I finished my presentation and headed for the stairs, the backstage lights went off and I fell off the bloody stage!

Every day is the way

Attaining goals is easier if you break big goals up into smaller ones. Apply a realistic daily routine that eliminates unproductive activities and maximises performance. It's not about big changes every month. It's about small changes every day. This way, every day is a stepping stone in your progress and in your dedication to hitting your target. Success only comes through unqualified dedication to achieving goals.

BULLET POINTS

- Double the deadline and reach your goal.

- Never confuse activity with accomplishment.

- Be sure that the daily landscape doesn't put the horizon out of focus.

- Success doesn't come overnight; it comes over time.

- Solve problems – achieve goals.

- Persistence always defeats resistance.

- Every day is the way to achieving goals.

THE
BULLSEYE PRINCIPLE™

3 IMPLEMENT THE STRATEGY

TACTICS, TECHNIQUES, AND FUNDAMENTALS

Chapter 3
Winning or losing

BULLISM:™ WIN-A-BULL

You don't have to be the biggest to be the best.

Barry Bull

The *Bullseye Principle* is not just about business. It applies to most things in life and is particularly relevant to sport: at the playing field, pool, pitch, court, track or footy stadium. I was in the UK when Britain lost the Euro 2004 World Series soccer to France by one point in the last ninety seconds of the game. This devastated a nation and the whole country was in uproar for the next few days because they had lost in such a close contest. You would think it was World War III! However, there can only be one winner. The difference between winning and losing comes down to the team who can be the best on the day. And Beckham didn't bend it really well *that* day!

Two weeks later I was speaking in Hamilton, New Zealand, on a two-week business road show hosted by the New Zealand Retailers Association. Coincidentally, the conference room where I was speaking was at the same stadium where the All Blacks had beaten Argentina the day before. It is no secret that rugby is a religion to the Kiwis in the same way that soccer is sacred to the Europeans. The Kiwis were exhilarated with the spirit of winning; it was all they talked about for the next week. Because of this, my job as a motivational speaker was easy. They were *already* on fire! They really got into the spirit, however, when I arrived dressed 'all in black'. Timing is everything – right?

Being in both countries to witness the way nations need to embrace the spirit of winning reinforced something that I have always known. Being the best is not just a singular objective for each competitor. It influences the spirit of a team, a whole community and, sometimes, an entire nation. And when the Olympics are on: the whole world.

This is why I emphasise that *everyone* needs a goal, because deep down humanity has an instinct for competition and a need to succeed. If you doubt this, then why did millions of people in Europe and New Zealand react to their teams being the best? I must admit I felt more comfortable returning home and watching the Brisbane Lions roar at their competition at the 'Gabba. To me, nothing ignites Aussie passion more than good old Aussie Rules. Nevertheless, the passion that each nation feels as they watch their heroes is the whole reason for their heroes' success. This, in turn, inspires another generation of young achievers.

Now let's take these same values into your playing field, into your business, into your team. How can your performance affect others? I embrace the belief that you don't need to be the biggest to be the best. This simple belief is the reason for our continued success in our family business, which is not to say that expansion and growth should be stifled, in fact quite the opposite. We all need to grow to stay relevant, to cover increasing overheads and fend off competition. Notwithstanding this, every business is different and circumstances vary from industry to industry. My philosophy is not about the size of the business, it is about the size of the performance. Because, regardless of size, one thing remains the same – success demands being the best.

The difference between winning and losing can be so small it often comes down to little things that can affect the outcome of team performance (as the Brits discovered over their loss to France). As the song says, *little things mean a lot*, and they can add up to a lot of big things; often to the difference between winning and losing.

The spirit of winning is no greater than during the Olympics. The difference between winning and losing, between lifetime dreams being fulfilled or shattered, can come down to a fraction of a second. As the world watched the Athens 2004 games, the spirit of human excellence seemed stronger than ever before. Witnessing such extraordinary performance levels inspired a whole planet.

Whether it's the Olympics or your local footy team, don't just savour the entertainment value of these events. Be inspired to lift your personal performance levels no matter how big or small the endeavour. Set your goals. If you don't have a goal, then get one. You don't have to be the biggest to be the best, but by being the best, bigger will take care of itself. As we saw at the Olympics – *winners are recognised, rewarded and remembered.*

If it's the little things that make the difference, then let's look at some of the little things in business that we all know about. We may tend to overlook them, and they take constant vigilance to maintain. Whenever I am travelling and visit retail and service centres, I notice that basic principles are often overlooked or taken for granted. I call them *forgotten fundamentals*. These commonly made mistakes in retail compromise performance and hinder progress.

And, as you might expect, they all come with a Bullism.

Forgotten fundamentals

1. PRESENT-A-BULL

Don't devalue your brand by placing clearance goods or obsolete merchandise at the front of your store. It is beyond me why merchants believe that merchandise that can't be sold in store can be cleared at the store front. This is premium retail space. It will generate maximum dollars with current, relevant merchandise and is your highest (per square metre) rental cost if your store is in a shopping centre or mall. Also landlords in shopping centres dislike merchandise cluttering lease lines. They place significant value on the way retail store fronts contribute to the presentation of their shopping centre.

> **Fact file**: Frontages are the most valued asset in a shopping mall and rents are determined by the size of the frontage. This is why smaller tenancies can pay more rent pro-rata than tenants of larger premises.

Your store front is also your window to your customers and is the headline to your store. Don't clutter it. Instead, value it like an editor values a newspaper headline. Think about it. Readers scan headlines and decide if they are interested in reading the story. Headlines sell newspapers. Customers appraise your store in the same way and decide if they want to enter. If the store front is cluttered, confusing and sending the wrong message about your business, they will probably pass you by. Alternatively, if the store offers good merchandise they will be encouraged to come in for a browse.

2. BROWSE-A-BULL

Give your customers permission to browse. Allow them room to move and have clearly defined passageways for customers to wheel their shopping trolleys. That's right, shopping trolleys. Many retailers are in shopping malls that contain supermarkets and mall shoppers often have shopping trolleys. Some retailers have the misconception that they should fill as much space as possible with inventory because of the rental cost. This is false economy. Whenever you plan refurbishment, your first consideration should be easy access to inventory from the front to the back of the store. Giving customers permission to browse keeps them in the store longer and usually results in more sales.

Associated with this fundamental is allowing your customers counter access. Counter clutter is a common mistake found in many service centers. Give your customer space for their merchandise, to choose their credit card and feel comfortable as they make their transaction. Counter space is also a valuable merchandising area for add-on sales, so pay attention to what goes on at the counter. Remember it should be like the kitchen table: clean and tidy at all times, and set to serve.

These fundamentals also apply to web browsing: web sites that sell allow browsers to navigate easily, offer information and choice, and make purchasing easy.

3. TOUCH-A-BULL

Give your customers permission to touch the merchandise. Good retailers know that once merchandise is in the customer's hand it's hard to give back. The emotion of ownership is highest at this point so make merchandise accessible. A friend of mine is a veteran jeweller and she knows that once a ring goes on the finger or a necklace around the neck, it is difficult to hand back. I never buy a business shirt without first trying it on. If it fits well and looks good I usually buy two. Always be aware of the power of the senses. The sense of touch, smell, sight and sound are powerful emotional triggers that ignite desire and ownership. They all contribute to the ambience and mood of the merchandising experience. It's a magic that some stores have and some don't.

4. MERCHANDISE-A-BULL

I was speaking in New Zealand recently and spent a weekend in Wellington. Now I know a weekend in Wellington sounds like a romantic line out of a travel brochure, but it was far from that. Whilst it is a beautiful city built on one of the best natural harbours in the world, it is well known that Wellington in winter can be windy and wet. The weekend I chose for R and R was no exception. I found myself in a bookstore looking for a good read to pass the time on this bleak weekend. However, the lighting levels were insufficient for me to read comfortably. I observed that there were plenty of lights but the illumination level was at fifty per cent performance because the fluorescent tubes needed replacing. To compound the problem the gloomy day outside added nothing to the lifeless atmosphere inside. If you cannot see the print in a bookstore what chance has the bookseller got? Talk about store blindness!

Up the road was another bookstore and, despite the grey weather, its illumination level made it look like Fiji! You know where I bought my book that day? The point I make is this: because we work in the same environment every day we tend not to see the wood for the trees. Our customers, however, certainly do. Effective lighting creates retail theatre and is a critical part of the merchandising offer.

Another of the essentials of effective merchandising is good signage. We want no handwritten signs, but professional computer-generated tickets that are easy to read (and easy to make these days with affordable printers). Just as importantly, write interesting merchandising messages. Whilst in this bookstore, I noticed some slick merchandising for the release of Bill Clinton's biography that demanded my attention. The merchandiser simply said *'Politics, Power and Really Good Sax!'*. This was clever advertising and very attention-grabbing, providing a creative sales message to a new bestseller. I grinned to myself, thinking that was a special Kiwi thing, because every time they say 'sax' or 'six', we all know what it sounds like!

4. UNFORGIVE-A-BULL

'What, you're out of stock!'

Nothing upsets customers more than a store running out of stock of bestsellers. This is one obvious weakness of mass marketers, and it's where a specialist can beat them. For an independent specialty merchant who sells on experience and not price, to be caught without stock of a bestseller is unforgivable. Time-poor customers don't necessarily buy on price, but on convenience and confidence. They will remain loyal to your business, if *they* know, *you* know, what *they* want, *when* they want it.

On the plane from Brisbane to New Zealand, I sat next to a really nice guy who was taking his wife and kids on a skiing holiday to Queenstown. Now I know this is starting to sound like I work for the New Zealand tourist bureau, but some of my best networking experiences come to me while I am travelling. He asked me my name because I looked familiar. I love it when people say that. It means that my crazy promotional activities are working. I told him I owned Toombul Music. 'That's where I've seen you,' he cried. 'I've been coming to your shop for years!' As I said, he was a really nice guy, saying all the right things. He told me he lived at Chandler, which is about thirty minutes away from our shop and he would pass half a dozen competitors to get to Toombul. Naturally this was music to my ears. Then he turned around to his wife in the seat behind him and said, 'Guess what? I'm sitting next to the guy who owns Toombul Music!' His wife retorted,

'We've spent a fortune with you over the years!'

While range is important the eighty/twenty principle must always be understood. Eighty per cent of sales come from twenty per cent of inventory. The challenge is, knowing *which* twenty per cent of inventory makes up the bestsellers. We are investment managers with stock and it is a bad investment if stock is not selling. Equally, it is bad investing to be out of the turnover titans. Identify the biggest sellers that constitute eighty per cent of sales and never be out of stock of these profit performers.

Importantly, if you can predict bestsellers early then you can get on the front end of a trend and ride the sales wave all the way to the beach. Early sales are the best because you get in before the competition. Just like surfing early in the morning, you can have the waves to yourself. If you surf the rising tide, the result can often be the most rewarding. The most exhilarating ride of all, however, is on the rogue big one – the one others don't see coming. If you're prepared, then that's where the biggest sales are.

Over the years a few big ones come to mind and we got in early and rode them all the way. We recognised the potential of the CD back in 1986 and were quick to see that DVDs were another memorable shift in technology. Artists like The Corrs, Nora Jones and Sir Cliff's 'The Millennium Prayer' (more about that later) were all trends we recognised and ran with. They all became bestsellers for us long before our competition caught on.

Don't get caught out with no stock. Stock depth is far better than stock width, so never be out of the good sellers. The easiest way to lose a customer for life is to disappoint them when they least expect it.

———

Here is a story which I am sure will strike a chord.

It's a hot day at the beach and you head for the cola machine. Its refreshing 'ice-cold' signage is a clever and compelling vending message. You stick in your two bucks and nothing happens. The goddamn machine is either out of product or your money is stuck. Either way you lose. Apart from wanting to choke this money-munching machine, you may never go back to the brand.

There is one of those self-serve car washes not far from where I live. You know the kind, where you stick in the money and then wash your vehicle yourself. I visited it usually on the weekend when most people have the time to perform this menial task. Generally there is no attendant. Why would you want an attendant at the busiest time of the week? On this occasion I put in my ten bucks and nothing happened. The money needed clearing because it was a busy weekend and the coin receptacle had jammed. After much poking and pulling, trying to retrieve my coins, I gave up and left a note in the suggestion box that they owed me ten bucks! I also gave my telephone number. Nothing happened. About a month later I returned to the same car wash (on a weekend) and the same thing happened again.

Apart from never using this facility again I have told this story so many times that it wouldn't surprise me if it closed down. Now I am a reasonable bloke and am always prepared to give a second chance, but when the customer service people have a chance to redeem themselves and fail miserably, then there can be no sympathy for stupidity.

On a positive note, however, this is not always the case. Recently I arranged to meet a colleague for a business meeting in one of the private conference rooms in the Qantas Club at the Brisbane airport. Although we booked the room in advance, when I arrived my colleague informed me that there were no rooms available. Our alternative was to find a quiet spot in the general club lounge. Qantas had stuffed up and we were not impressed. Within thirty minutes we received a written letter of apology, hand delivered by the Qantas customer-relations supervisor apologising for the inconvenience they had caused. They informed us that by presenting this letter at any Qantas lounge in the future we could have *free* access to a conference room. Now that wasn't too difficult was it?

It's all very well to get the chocolates on the pillow, but if service values aren't followed through then that will probably be the last time you use the facility.

There is an old retail chestnut that says: *Take care of your customers or someone else will.*

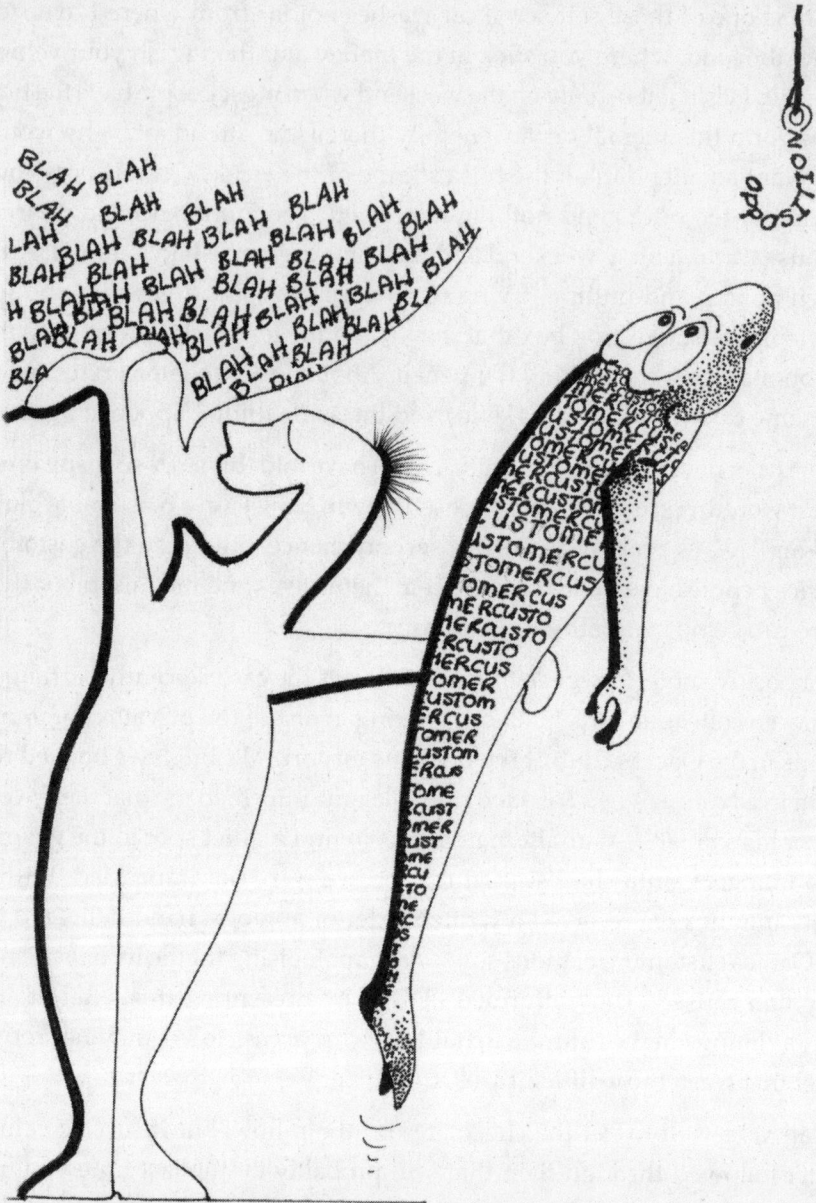

Take care of your customers or someone else will.

5. CONTACT-A-BULL

Smile and the whole world smiles with you.

A great lyric from an evergreen classic song with a timeless message. I've always believed that a smiling face in retail gives a happy result at the bottom line. The most valuable salespeople are those who are happy and continually show it. I believe that you have two minutes to sell yourself. To allow your customers to like you, trust your advice and convince them to buy from you. A warm and friendly smile is the icebreaker that often seals the deal.

Just as important as a smile is eye contact. Look your customers in the eye and they will feel that they are the only customer that matters. Train the team to smile and make eye contact with everyone who enters your store, even though they may not be able to approach them immediately. It sends a clear message – 'Welcome to our business, we know you are there and we are here to assist'. And it also sends a message to potential shoplifters – 'I'm watching you so don't even think about it!'

Customer contact is fundamental to making a sale. Why retailers with sizable tenancies choose to position their sales counter at the back of their shop baffles me. My strategy has always been face to face customer contact, which is why our service counter is at the front of our store. The first thing a customer sees when they enter is an interested smiling person who greets them. This positioning puts us in control of traffic flow and strengthens customer awareness.

There's an old remedy for people who can't smile – fake it till you make it!

All good housekeeping is a daily routine. Every morning when you arrive at work, make your first task a tour of duty. Look for the little things before they become big problems and ensure that the fundamentals aren't forgotten.

BULLET POINTS

🔫 You don't need to be the biggest to be the best.

🔫 It's not about the size of the business it's about the size of the performance.

🔫 Winners are recognised, rewarded and remembered.

🔫 Forgotten fundamentals – the little things that mean a lot.

🔫 Loyalty is when *they* know, *you* know, what *they* want, *when* they want it.

🔫 Stock depth before stock width.

🔫 Take care of your customers or someone else will.

Chapter 4
Manage your margins

BULLISM™: PROFIT-A-BULL

Capitalise – don't cannibalise.

Barry Bull

N ow that we've dealt with the forgotten fundamentals, what about the importance of margin management? Margin is the difference between the cost of goods or services and what the consumer pays for them. So many businesses lose sight of the reason they are in business. That is to make a profit. The more I talk to business people today the more stressed they become about margin erosion due to competition. Well let me tell you, it's not going to get any better! As competition increases, margin pressure becomes a real concern as big business chases volume.

It all started back in the sixties with Wal-Mart. Although they are regarded with admiration as the world's largest retailer, their policy of 'best prices every day' began a price spiral that was to result in a world of shrinking margins. Although Wal-Mart are not in Australia, their business model of 'best prices' has been adopted by most Australian mass-market chains. With the increase in the number of retailers who are now public companies, the pressure is on to perform to their profit projections, published in their prospectuses. As soon as the market hiccups, the 'on-sale' siren becomes their only salvation.

The consequence of driving prices down is that margins go down too, but rents and operating costs continue to rise. With margins continuing to decline and property developers driving occupancy costs upwards, it's easy to see why profitability is under pressure in most sectors of today's marketplace.

There is no such thing as a level playing field, however, particularly for smaller businesses. Major department retailers that are anchor tenants for landlords are offered long-term leases with reduced occupancy costs due to their large tenancy requirement and market power. Conversely smaller businesses often get the opposite deal: shorter lease terms and occupancy costs that subsidise the major tenancies. Majors sell for less because of these advantages which drives volume. With volume come more advantages. They negotiate privileged volume rebate terms from their suppliers which subsidises their margin shortfall. This then puts margin pressure on suppliers so the whole supply chain gets leaner, and so on it goes. Everyone is therefore chasing margins.

Hardly seems fair, does it, if you are in a small-to-medium-size enterprise? The answer is not to compete or you will get run over. It's no good taking on the big guy. It's like not giving way to the semi on the highway – he's the king of the road and size matters. But you can't just stop in the middle of the road. You will also get run over. The answer is to go another way. Find your own highway. The big difference, however, between smaller business and big business – is you! You can build relationships with your clients; big business finds this more difficult.

So let's look at my Bullism strategies which deal with profit protection.

1. CHARGE-A-BULL

Create, don't compete; innovate don't imitate.

Be creative with your product offer so you're not competing with the big end. Be innovative in your marketing so you are offering something different.

Don't get carried away with volume. *Sell less for more!* Make sure every sale is profitable and concentrate on specialising in inventory that the price predators don't stock. This doesn't mean not stocking branded demand products. Customers want these, but they can often be the leanest profit performers.

If you integrate into your inventory mix a diversified product range that is specialised and contains more margin, this will assist to increase the average profit per item and your overall gross profit (gross profit is the margin between sales and cost of goods).

The way to achieve this is to be selective with your product and your suppliers. Work up business plans with suppliers who are chasing margins just like you and who don't sell to the mass marketers. Always have a preferred supplier list and use it. These are the people that you spend your negotiating time with. Have a win-win attitude. Support their product and give merchandising commitment to their range in return for an enhanced gross margin. The purpose of good business partnership is to increase mutual gross profits.

Gross profit is the only performance result that matters and is the key to a profitable business. Gross profit is the holy grail in the business of buying and selling. Landlords know this and many rental benchmarks are based on the average gross margin of their tenant's business. (That's right, we don't all pay the same rental rate.)

The greater the margin you make per sale the more gross profit you have to apply to the bottom line to cover fixed overheads and expenses. Whatever is left after overheads and tax is yours. If you don't make sufficient gross profit to cover these fixed expenses you get nothing. Now as fundamental as this may seem, the difference between a profit and loss in a fiscal year can come down to a few percentage points on the gross profit ledger. It's amazing the difference your profit result will be if *every* day you add a couple of points to the gross profit percentage of *every* sale. Progress is not necessarily about big changes. It's about small changes every day.

There are two ways to do this.

Firstly – buy right

The price you pay for your investment always determines the return on investment. Isn't this true in property and share market investments? So why not inventory investments? I manage our business inventory investment in the same way as I manage all other investments in our portfolio.

One way to secure favourable purchasing arrangements is to enter into an annual business plan with preferred suppliers and negotiate incentive purchasing terms for volume rebates. The easiest way to match big business's purchasing power is to join an industry buying group or a branded cooperative.

Secondly – charge right

Establish a fair and reasonable value for your goods and services, and charge for your time and experience. If you are selling specialised products and offering your time as a consultant, then charge for your experience. Your price reflects your level of experience, expertise and service. You can't be the cheapest in town and offer superior experience and knowledge.

There are two kinds of businesses – price driven and experience driven. If you're in the price-driven business then price is your only master. Who's closest to the customer and who has the best price? But if you're in the experience-driven business then people will pay for good advice and service. Granted, some won't, but do you want them as customers anyway? If your price is fair and your experience allows you to give superior service, people will pay the price. These are the customers you want because they are the profitable ones. The key is to reward them, retain them and ask for referrals.

Beware of giving away those extra margin points. If you must in order to remain competitive, then make sure that by product diversification and range, other sales make up the difference, so the average gross profit target is attained. The way to do this is to support the popular products that have leaner margins (the turnover titans) with less popular products that have a greater margin. A balanced average margin strategy that combines lower margin sales with higher margin products will give an acceptable average gross profit.

It's also important to know how much average gross profit covers overheads and provides an acceptable return on investment. This has to be your target. The most important fundamental in our business is watching the gross profit average because you will be amazed at the difference a few percentage points can make. If you give them away by competing on price you are giving your hard-earned profit opportunities away. Equally the difference that a few extra profit points make can be the difference between failure and success. Or, in lifestyle terms, which is the way many think, the difference between a camping holiday and an overseas trip of your dreams.

Many people, particularly those in smaller businesses, are struggling to improve bottom-line profit results. Many are going backwards trying to compete with the big business pressure on prices that make margins really tight. Others are keeping their profit results acceptable while facing increasing overheads.

How would you like to *double* your profit result? In the following chart you will see a formula to do this, using a business with annual gross sales of $5 000 000 and fixed costs, including rent, wages and other operating costs, totalling $1 500 000. The only variable amount is the gross profit, expressed as a percentage of sales.

Column (1) = 35% gross profit

Column (2) = 36% gross profit

Column (3) = 40% gross profit

See the difference to the bottom line that a 5% increase in your gross profit percentage can make.

	1 35% GP	2 36% GP	3 40% GP
Sales	5 000 000	5 000 000	5 000 000
Gross profit	1,750 000	1 800 000	2 000 000
Direct costs	1 000 000	1 000 000	1 000 000
Overhead costs	500 000	500 000	500 000
Net profit	$250 000	$300 000	$500 000
Gross profit %	35%	36%	40%
Increase in gross profit %		1%	5%
Increase in net profit %		20%	100%

Column 1 is the base result.

Column 2 shows that a 1% increase in gross profit % results in a 20% increase in net profit over column 1.

Column 3 shows that a 5% increase in gross profit % results in a 100% increase in net profit over column 1.

Fact file: The 1% rule, using column 1 in the above example. If you increase sales by 1%, decrease cost of goods sold by 1%, decrease overhead expenses by 1% and decrease direct costs by 1%, the net profit increases by 39%.

The result of discounting

If you discount your product, which reduces gross profit, the above process will reverse.

- a 1% decrease in gross profit per cent results in a 20% decrease in net profit from column 1.

- a 5% decrease in gross profit per cent results in a 100% decrease in net profit from column 1.

As you can see by the above exercise, a 5% reduction in the gross profit percentage would result in a zero net profit. This is why discounting is dangerous. So beware of the four-letter word – SALE. It can easily mean – sell more for less! Discounting is the most overdone marketing strategy to attract customers and increase turnover. So before you attempt to match a competitor's prices, you need to understand the effect this will have on the bottom line. If discounting, however, is a strategy to improve cash flow, then be careful. Discounting creates a leveraged impact on profits and can result in the business trading at below the break-even threshold.

Fact file: Using the above example of 35% gross profit, if selling price is discounted by 10%, sales volume needs to increase by 40% to maintain profit level. If selling price is discounted by 20% (which is nothing unusual these days), then sales volume needs to increase by 133% just to maintain the same profit position.

We are not talking big increments here yet small positives or negatives to the gross profit make a *big* difference to the bottom line

Profit control

I have kept this example simple because each business has its own turnover thresholds and each industry has its own margin and cost structures. So check this with your accountant; he or she can fill in any gaps so that this applies to your business. The principle is the same. Sell products that are profitable, contain costs and improve sales. Business is not difficult when you can see at a glance your bottom-line budget forecasts. It becomes difficult, however, if we prioritise the wrong things; like focussing on the top line (sales) and not on the bottom line (profit). I have five simple rules for profit control.

    1. Supplier support (rebates and cooperative advertising)

    2. Inventory Control

    3. Minimise operating costs

    4. Maximise gross profit

    5. Increase sales

Supplier Support
Inventory Control
Minimise Operating Costs
Maximise Gross Profit
Increase Sales
Profit

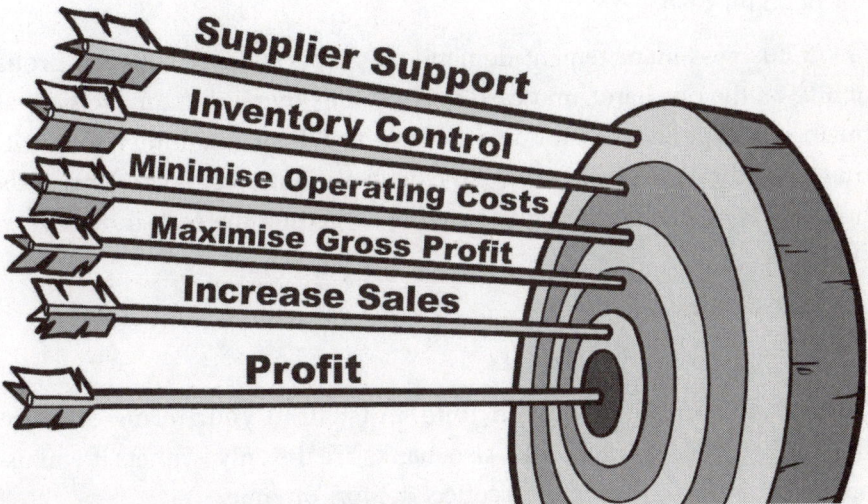

Maintain a pricing policy that is consistently profitable. Create, don't compete; add value, don't cut valuable margins; and buy right. Profitability is not only *the* most important element in the business plan – it's the very reason *for* the business plan.

There is one other important ingredient in the financial mix: appreciating the value of cash flow.

2. VALUE-A-BULL

Just as blood carries the rhythm of life in the human body, so cash flow is the life blood of business. Cash flow is the income stream that flows through your business from sales, billings, etc., after deducting outgoings (fixed overheads, variable expenses and creditors).

I am sure we all have, at some stage, listened to our accountant tell us that we are making good profits, yet we have asked ourselves with some concern, *'Where is it? Show me the money!'*

One thing is certain. A business can never grow faster than its cash allows. It's important to understand the difference between profit and cash flow. A business that is profitable won't necessarily have a good cash flow. Equally, a business with good cash flow may not always be profitable. Failure to control debtors and inventory can result in a profitable business being strapped for cash.

Good business management demands a proper balance between profitability on the one hand, and cash flow on the other. From time to time all businesses experience cash-flow problems and there is nothing wrong with that, providing the gross profit of the business is strong and healthy. If the business is profitable then it is a matter of getting the cash-flow rhythm right.

Here are five ways to do this.

1. Keep tight control of debtors

Collect outstanding funds on time and within your terms of trade. Remember you are not a bank. Also, banks are the only winners if you use an overdraft facility and fail to collect debtors on time.

If you provide credit then make sure your payment terms are clearly stated on your invoice, which should also include a late payment charge.

2. Use your creditors' trading terms to the max

Try to ensure that you have been paid for inventory or services before you pay your suppliers. For example, say you receive thirty-day trading terms from your suppliers. This means all goods purchased during any given month are due for payment at the end of the following month. If you can plan to purchase the bulk of your month's stock on the *first day* of the new trading month, you effectively have sixty days in which to pay for that inventory. This means that if you turn your stock every two months (six times a year), then you have sold this stock by the time settlement is due. As a result, your suppliers are funding your inventory and not your bank (via an overdraft). There's a big difference. Because you are working within the trading terms of your supplier you are saving bank overdraft interest charges. This frees up cash to do other things and reduces bank debt.

Additionally, if you can negotiate early payment terms with your suppliers (and if your cash flow allows it), then settlement discounts go straight to the bottom line, and the gross profit immediately improves. This is one way you can increase your gross profit percentage those extra couple of points as illustrated earlier. It just requires smarter management of money and inventory.

Importantly, keep these rebates separate and don't inflate the profit of your individual stock items. This extended margin can easily be given away by an exuberant sales team. I always show settlement rebates and incentive payments separate in my balance sheet. I earned this money. It is my bonus for negotiating favourable trading terms. It doesn't apply to sales staff commission arrangements.

This discipline assists cash flow and takes pressure off the overdraft. The interest saved is a bonus. Interest rates on business loans today are relatively moderate; however, I painfully remember the time when they climbed to eighteen per cent. That taught me a thing or two about inventory management! Which brings me to my next point.

3. Manage inventory

Don't pour all your profits back into stock. Purchases should equal the cost of goods sold. For example, if your sales for a month are $100 000 and your average gross profit is forty per cent, then your purchases for that month should average $60 000.

Monthly sales = $100 000

Gross profit at forty per cent = $40 000

Cost of goods = $60 000

This is where monthly sales *and* purchasing budgets are essential.

Also it's important to know your industry benchmark for stock turnover rates. The number of times you turn over your stock will have a significant effect on the profitability of the business. You'd be surprised at the number of businesses that fail to turn over their stock within an acceptable term. This fundamental issue has a major effect on the cash flow of the business. Too little stock and sales will suffer. Too much stock and cash flow suffers. Efficiency in business is about finding the right balance.

4. Forecast cashflow budgets each month

Just as you prepare sales and profit forecasts, it is essential to prepare cash flow forecasts. If you work on a thirty-day creditor's cycle, then it is critical to forecast projected income to meet creditor obligations when they fall due, as well as provide for all other fixed expenses including BAS payments. Since the introduction of the GST many businesses have lost their cash-flow rhythm through lack of monthly forecasting.

5. Watch your margins

Discounting is a sure way to make sales and maintain short-term cash flow. However, it eventually dries up because your gross profit is squeezed and therefore ultimately your equity in the business is reduced.

The rhythm of life in any business is cash flow. If you take your eye off it, then it is easy to lose. Value it and protect it, but most of all treat it as you

*Since the introduction of the GST many businesses have
lost their cash-flow rhythm.*

do inventory. It's simply a mechanism for trading goods and services and is a means to an end. However, lose it – and it could mean the end.

3. LEVERAGE-A-BULL

Another way to build profit is to develop the 'add-on' sale. Every business has core products and services: it's their reason for being in business; the reason customers come to them.

In many cases these core products or services are the very ones that may cause problems with profitability because of competition. It's like those bestsellers: they should never be out of stock, but they don't always support the best margins. They are, however, traffic builders and every business needs them. Newsagencies have newspapers, magazines and lotto as traffic generators, but their profitable lines like books, cards and stationery are a valuable part of the product mix. Pharmacies' core business is prescription medicine, even though it is the cosmetic and pharmaceutical retail services that provide sustainable margins. I could go on but I think you understand my point.

As I've said, profitable retailing and servicing is about how we use our core products or services to sell products with greater margins. It's important to develop a strategy to leverage off demand product to build sales of profitable product. It's also important to 'up-sell' or build extra sales while the customer is in store.

> **Fact file**: Say over a month you sold 1000 customers an extra item for just $5, at a gross profit margin of 40%. You have just added $2000 to the bottom line by this simple up-selling.

It's that easy! We do this every Christmas by offering our customers a small gift wrapper for their CD Christmas gift purchases. It puts profit onto the bottom line with very little extra effort because we are selling to the same customer. McDonald's understand this discipline better than most. They sensitively 'up-sell' into other product categories by providing a value-concept to their offer, while at the same time broadening their customers' perception of what's on their menu.

While up-selling is important, it's also smart to leverage off an established brand to build future business through diversification. Every business needs diversification to survive.

Australia Post does this very well. How would you like to have 1 000 000 customers a day? Australia Post is Australia's largest retail network with 4400 outlets nationwide – an impressive retail distribution network. Because of this, they leverage off their core products – such as traditional postal services, bill paying, etc. – into cards, toys, stationery, books and calendars, all products you would not expect to see in a post office. They have a good reason to offer more choice to their considerable customer base, and cleverly use their traditional postal services, which attract huge customer traffic, to expose other retail products and electronic services, thereby creating new add-on sales. This is a classic case of leveraging off a traditional brand and using core competencies to 'up-sell' and develop future business. If you're thinking this is another example of big business getting bigger, you are partly right, except that over sixty per cent of Australia Post outlets are operated under licence, many by small family enterprises.

The important lesson here is that nothing is for ever and leveraging off core business not only increases the average sale today, but builds new business for tomorrow.

When I first met my accountant twenty years ago we were one of his first clients. In those days he concentrated on my tax returns and end-of-year financials. Today his business incorporates consultancy, training, financial advisor services, superannuation management and a host of other professional services that have leveraged off traditional core competencies.

How long can you depend on your core business to continue? Look at how the digital camera has changed the photographic industry. Kodak expected film sales to last for ever. With today's digital technology, however, film processing might well become a thing of the past.

Look at the music industry. How would you like to be in a business whose core product can be obtained for free? Illegal CD downloads via the internet are a real problem for the music industry as broadband services expand and convergence increases between mobile phones and wireless networks.

Am I saying our business is also threatened by this shift in distribution? Absolutely! It all depends, however, on how you define change. What is your attitude towards competition that is beyond your control? The answer is to take control (of your destiny).

Realise that *change is not a threat – it's an opportunity.*

Music and video formats have evolved many times over the past fifty years. I am fortunate to have gained experience from living through these technological changes. As a very young boy, I listened to my grandfather's cylinder gramophone, and watched my parents create their own home entertainment using the 'miracle' of piano rolls from a pedal-pumping piano called a pianola. When I entered the music industry at fifteen, the seventy-eight rpm shellite record was being replaced by the forty-five rpm single, and the microgroove long-play record. When I acquired Toombul Music, one of my early initiatives was to introduce the first CDs to Brisbane, which quickly replaced the LP record and eventually the cassette. The DVD has now replaced the VHS tape and has breathed new life into home entertainment, creating the home cinema.

All of these technological shifts provided opportunity for growth, because each new technology leveraged off the DNA of the former. Traditional formats were transformed to provide a more convenient and improved audio and video carrier to a techno-hungry consumer.

The same is true of internet technology. While on-line technology will provide more global competition and allow for broader distribution channels, it also allows traditional merchants to leverage off their individual core competencies to find their niche in this new world. Our on-line philosophy is predictably: *create don't compete, innovate don't imitate,* and use unique core products and services to broaden retail distribution services. We can source music from around the globe more efficiently, thus providing a better service for our customers. We can also provide unique personally autographed product (as a result of our frequent artist presentations) to our on-line VIP Club customers, wherever they live. And we can reach 500 Cliff Richard fans with a single touch of an email transmission button.

It's all about leveraging off an established brand that is known for its core products, and then seizing opportunities to diversify.

Over the years we diversified our business into musical products, sheet music, DVDs, consumer electronics and most recently home cinema. Leveraging off our strong brand enabled us to hedge against the slumps in the market and margin erosion of our traditional core products. It also allowed us to build new businesses with wider margins. We did this off one set of overheads so all that mattered was that our margins didn't fall as the market changed.

It's all a question of leveraging and averaging; develop a strategy to leverage off a brand renowned for traditional goods and services; build sales of more profitable products to increase the average margin and introduce new business by seizing new trends.

While CDs are on the back end of a trend, DVDs, satellite and digital television are at the front end of a new trend. The 'smart home' is being cabled for complete home automation with home cinema, security, communication, data and internet solutions, all with integrated computer controlled navigation. This is our new highway and the road's not crowded. Once a new opportunity emerges, the key is to market at the front end of the trend and establish a niche before the competition's traffic crowds your highway.

Research shows that seventy per cent of people go shopping without knowing what to buy. Good retailers know how to solve their problem.

BULLET POINTS

- Create don't compete, innovate don't imitate.

- Sell less for more.

- The price you pay for your investment always determines the return on investment.

The three objectives to customer targeting are: reward, retain and referral.

Small positives or negatives to the gross profit make a *big* difference to the bottom line.

Change is not a threat – it's an opportunity.

A business can never grow faster than its cash allows.

Cash flow is a means to an end. But lose it, and it could mean the end.

Chapter 5

Hearing or listening

BULLISM:™ LISTEN-A-BULL

In the past our customers were loyal to us because they knew us. In the future they will only be loyal if we know them.

Retail chestnut

Too much competition and too much choice weaken traditional loyalties. Just as the gap is widening between the 'haves' and the 'have-nots', so the gap is expanding between big business and all other businesses. Smaller businesses suffer most from consumers switching loyalty and are most vulnerable to globalisation. They are bullied by big business and are unfairly penalised by regulations and discrimination.

As those at the big end of town accelerate their diversification into specialty goods and services, the traditional domain of independent businesses is under increasing threat. Major supermarket chains have migrated into liquor and petrol retailing and just about everything else while banks now offer wealth-management services. It is clear that the big end of town won't be satisfied until it owns the whole town, as corporate capitalising creeps into every corner of our daily lives.

Is it because the big end of town has more power and resources? Or is it that as markets expand smaller businesses need to 'stick to their knitting' and do what they do best, provide better service? Smaller businesses certainly need to understand how globalisation and technology are changing their world and adapt to this change.

As alluded to earlier, the power retail game began in the sixties in the US with retail giant Wal-Mart. Their slogan, 'always lower prices', drove prices down in almost every retail category. They have earned their reputation as the world's largest retailer. Wal-Mart now sells the most sporting goods and jewellery in the US, as well as the most CDs and DVDs. They are fast becoming the leader in furnishings and electronics and are the largest food and grocery retailer. They even sell Fender electric guitars!

They are the category killer extraordinaire, and now have their sights set on an annual global turnover of US$1 trillion.

Wal-Mart's success has come from offering products at lower prices than their rivals at the expense of customer service and fancy fit-outs. But lower prices also mean lower margins. Rival discount chains that concentrated on competing with Wal-Mart came unstuck, as K-Mart US discovered.

Fortunately there are many retail success stories in the US which tell of businesses happily coexisting with this turnover titan. By not following a price-driven model, they go about building a specialised brand, underpinning their offer with experience and service.

There are two kinds of retailers, price driven and experience driven. Commonly linked to these models are the two 'V' words, *volume* and *value*. The key is to know where you want to be, which business you want to be in and which 'V' word applies to your business model. Some businesses have no idea where they want to be and consequently have no idea who *their* customer is.

I have always known that I was in the experience business and positioned our brand image around specialisation and elite customer service. Experience-driven retailers can coexist with price-driven category killers chasing volume, providing they target their customers and offer value. The mass marketers don't usually win on person-to-person experience or store experience – and that's where the 'specialists' can win.

A discerning, time-poor consumer will happily spend more if they can get service and don't have to climb ladders or walk up aisles looking for something while being overwhelmed by range. You can charge a premium for your product providing you add value to your service. Value is not just price. It is product differentiation, information and presentation and all this adds value to your customers' experience. Importantly, the real value is gaining your customers' loyalty.

So here lies the long-term objective for specialty business. Create a brand loyalty, which builds repeat business. We all know that repeat business is the most profitable. The secret to all this (and it must be a secret because so many fail to discover it) is know your customer: what they want, why they want it and when they want it. If you are still asking how – it's by *listening* to them.

One of the most important skills in selling is not too much telling ... it's *listening*. God gave us two ears and one mouth. Was he giving us a hint that listening is more important than talking? It is often said that listening is the most undervalued of the communication skills. People on average listen with less than fifty per cent efficiency and with a very short attention span. They only hear what they want to hear! There's a big difference between hearing and listening. Keep the volume turned up and listen to what your customer is saying (or not saying). When it's your turn to speak, ask your customer questions that will assist you to meet their needs. Then *shut up* and *listen* to their reply! *Selling* is sixty per cent listening and forty per cent *telling*!

This is why the traditional department store has struggled in recent years. They lost customer loyalty because they weren't listening. They didn't conform to value pricing and they lacked specialisation. They got caught between the discounters and the specialists.

Their research showed a need to reposition between the two. By combining pricing values to a more specialised product range their performance notably improved. This market repositioning, however, will threaten specialty retailers who target similar mid-range merchandise.

It is interesting to observe one of Australia's iconic department stores now struggling for market relevance. Could it be that they have lost sight of who their customers were or, more probably, their customers have lost sight of

Bottom-line profits.

them? By withdrawing traditional service values and introducing check-out queues, it is easy to lose traditional customer loyalties in order to meet cost-cutting objectives, even though you are successfully downsizing.

'Downsizing' is the new buzz word so be prepared for radical changes in the future as large corporations continually strive for more bottom-line profits to please an ever more demanding stock-market driven board. Companies are merging to seek economies of scale, and furthermore as technology replaces people, human resources become the big casualty. The irony is that IT personnel are increasing at the expense of service personnel.

Corporations are rapidly withdrawing their traditional customer support services as well as transferring labour costs to the consumer by offering concessions to use on-line electronic services. If you doubt this then look what electronic banking has done for banks. The friendly bank teller could be a thing of the past. It's getting harder to talk to a human voice on the phone as, more and more, big business share their costs with their customers. The electronic voice mail says: 'Your call is important to us.' And I yell: *'Well why don't you answer it?'*

If this is the trend then there are big opportunities for niche merchants to offer good old customer service. The harder it is to find, the more the customers appreciate it when they get it.

Just repeating that old retail saying, 'Take care of your customer, or someone else will.' This is a chestnut that has profound consequences for those who don't listen to their customers. So if you're like me in specialty business, and customer loyalty is everything, then 'stick to your knitting'. Don't focus on being the biggest in your category – just the best! *Where your focus goes – your energy flows.*

Listen to the whispers before you get the shouts.

Lazaris

BULLET POINTS

- There are two types of businesses – price driven and experience driven. Decide which one you're in.

- To charge a premium for your product you must add value to your service.

- Selling is sixty per cent *listening* and forty per cent *telling*!

- There are big differences between hearing and listening.

- Learn how to listen to your customer rather than speak unnecessarily just to be heard.

- Where your focus goes – your energy flows.

Chapter 6

Good service or great service

BULLISM™: CARE-A-BULL

If you treat your regular clients like your best friends, they will quickly become your best customers.

Barry Bull

So what is it that distinguishes good service from great service? Why is it that some businesses have great customer loyalty and their shops are always busy, regardless of competition? The one common value that these businesses share is that they regard customer service as the 'holy grail'.

Commerce today is out of control; excessive trading hours, administration in overload, too much competition and choice, an excess of everything, except the one thing that we all want most – service. Is it any wonder that the business that gets its service values in place is the place of value to its customers?

The road to success, however, is always under construction and continual refinement of the service offer is what makes great businesses powerful.

The power of customer connection is at its most potent on the shop floor, with the sales team. Management must train its people to meet and greet every customer who walks into their business – if this is not always possible then welcome them with your eyes. Look them *in the eyes*, and *smile*. It's so

It's so easy to make people feel welcome.

easy to make people feel welcome; *please – acknowledge them*! They don't have to be there. Use body language that lets them know they are welcome and you are pleased that they chose your store. I spend as much time coaching people about happy body language (like smiling) as I do teaching them to sell!

When you meet a customer for the first time you have only minutes to make that magic connection. The first impression is always the most important impression, so smile, and be yourself, because you are being judged by your customer as you greet them. If you sell yourself first you will have no problem in selling your product. In fact, if you sell yourself you will have no problem selling *anything* after that.

When a new employee starts, I tell them three things on their very first day. Sell *yourself* first, then sell the product, then sell the stability of our store brand. Then you can talk about price, which becomes less important, because you haven't done what most salespeople do, and that is to make price the issue, the reason to buy. By winning your customer's confidence you will win the price objection *every time*!

Have you ever considered why charismatic politicians are so successful? They know how to sell themselves. When being interviewed they look straight at the camera and you get the feeling they are talking just to you. Their ability to sound credible depends on how well they sell themselves. Neglecting this is the reason why many fail.

Let me explain this in another context.

My three rules of selling are:

Rule 1 – Sell yourself

Rule 2 – Get their attention

Rule 3 – Ask for the order

Most weeks I present at a conference somewhere in Australia. I am engaged to motivate, and take my message to *everyone* in the audience, and my challenge is to keep them attentive every minute of my one-hour presentation. Impossible, you might think, when my average audience is around 200 people and a person's average attention span is two minutes! Not really, because, remember, my profession is selling, and I was a salesman long before I stepped onto the public podium.

One of the *first* rules I learnt about selling was to sell yourself *first*. Make the customer comfortable and receptive to your sales presentation. What is the one thing that most customers do when they first encounter a sales-person? They put up a defensive barrier, a brick wall, right? A well-trained salesperson knows how to sell themselves to break that barrier.

When I am introduced to an audience I begin by selling myself and I know I have two minutes to do it. I start with a cheeky, humorous story that instantly grabs attention; this allows my audience to decide if they will listen to me. And down comes the brick wall! I know if I can get audience attention in the first two minutes, I have got them for the next fifty-eight! Once I have sold myself I then proceed to keep their attention by eyeballing *everyone* in the audience. That's right! I endeavour to look at *every* pair of eyes so they know I am speaking directly to them. This is my number two rule. If you have their attention you have a strong chance of selling your message.

If you have an audience in the palm of your hand then that's the place they want to be. They have to enjoy your presentation and they must feel comfortable with you. At the end of my presentation I suggest to my audience that if they want more information about my business principles, they should read my books. I cheekily tell them that I just happen to have some with me! What would they expect – I'm a *retailer*! Consequently, I sell a lot of books.

Rule 3 – *Don't* return home with a case full of books!

It is the same principle on the selling floor. People love to be sold to, otherwise they wouldn't be in your shop. My three salesmanship rules were taught to me when I was a trainee retailer at Kings, way back in the sixties. They worked then and they still work now. Do you know why? It's because I care about our business, I care about our service and most of all – I care about our customers. Our customers have been returning to our store for the past twenty-five years. Kids became teenagers, teens became adults, and many became our customers because of the simple connections formed by customer service. By treating our regulars like our best friends, they became our best customers.

People not places

The real wealth of our enterprise is not the money, nor the places I visit, but the wonderful human relationships that continue to evolve and mature every day, no matter where I go. And because I value these connections, somehow that brings out the best in these relationships.

Life is all about relationships. The world would be a boring place if we couldn't share our interests and passions with others. I've come to the realisation that the only thing that really matters is the relationships I've built with people. Whether its family, friends, customers, staff, audiences or suppliers, their long-term trust and my relationship with them are what really matter. If you want a rewarding career, one that is memorable, filled with enjoyment and lots of friendships, then the word *integrity* becomes vital.

I have a big issue here because the world lacks integrity. As the want for more increases so the want is fed. Friendships are abused, business relationships are dissolved, disloyalty and indiscretion shatter long-term trust between partners, all for the sake of selfishness and greed.

Integrity produces a world of honour, trust, loyalty and care which is in stark contrast to a world of fear. I remember the time when we could leave home without locking our doors. Today our security systems resemble something out of a Bond movie. We are fearful of our security, and much of what we do in life is driven by fear. What if this? What if that? We spend our lives 'boxing at shadows', fighting a foe that doesn't necessarily exist.

Our business has benefited greatly over the years from having strong principles of loyalty and trust. You must maintain these values if you expect them in return. I am attracted to people who cherish these same values.

Recently Cliff Richard released his best album in years. I contacted his UK office in the hope that he would do a live interview with me to promote his new product to his Aussie fans. The answer came back that he was out of the country and it was unlikely that he would be available. It didn't look good. Cliff is a man of great integrity and has returned my loyalty many times over the years. He surrounds himself with people who share his values. Within the week Cliff was on the phone from London to do my interview. This confirmed my belief that he knew that my efforts for him would demonstrate his loyalty to his Aussie fans.

No amount of ability is of the slightest avail without honour.

Andrew Carnegie

BULLET POINTS

- The business that gets its service values in place is the place of value for its customers.

- If you sell yourself you will have no problem selling *anything* after that.

- Integrity produces a world of honour, trust, loyalty and care.

Chapter 7

Effective branding builds market share

BULLISM™: RECOGNISE-A-BULL

If you don't have a brand you are a commodity; if you are a commodity then price is your only master.

Barry Bull

Effective branding builds market share. But good branding is not just a share of the market, it is a share of the mind. The prominence and positioning of your brand in the minds of your customers will influence how they make their decisions and how they spend their money. Brand recognition and trust support the value of the goods and services behind the brand.

To build a brand, you must understand what market you are in. There are two types of markets, mass market and niche market; or put another way, the price-driven business, or the experience-driven business. If you are in the business of promoting high-profile manufacturer's brands, then you are in the price-driven business and price is your only master. If you are in specialty business providing consultation, service and specialty products, then you are in the experience business.

There is no point in competing with the mass marketers because that war will only be won on price and convenience; the cheapest price at the nearest location. This is why it is so important to differentiate between your specialty business (with its goods and service values, its point of difference and the uniqueness of the product offered) and a mass marketer. If your customer cannot differentiate between you and your competitor, they will make a choice based on price not value.

Let me put it another way. Success in business requires repeated sales of consumable products or services. The successful businesses I admire the most are those that sell highly consumable products, which have a unique shopping experience attached to the merchandising. Each time I visit the USA I marvel at their creative brand development and the successful businesses that have been built from 'idea merchandising'. They are creating a point of difference in the world's most competitive retail marketplace. Retailers like The Gap, Williams and Sonoma, The Pottery Barn, Crate and Barrel, Ikea, and Victoria's Secret are examples of successful businesses selling consumable products that people want to buy. What makes them different or unique is the shopping experience they provide to their customers.

Regardless of the merchandise category or the type of business, these retail icons all seem to have similar agendas. I suspect this is the secret to their success. Their customer mission statement is clearly defined in their merchandising and supported by a perpetual employee training program. Their product and service offer is targeted differently from the competition. While merchandised superbly, their products are uniquely marketed using a recognisable brand. Here's the point to all of this. If you have a unique merchandising offer matched with the same service values, this is the difference needed to coexist with the mass marketers who just sell on price. This is how I have learned my craft. Travelling to the best retail precincts in the world and studying the mission statements of the stores within those precincts has helped me to understand the fundamentals of brand retailing. These retailers understand the influence their brands have on their core customers because they package their branding statement with a unique selling proposition.

Effective branding builds market share

Do you have a unique selling proposition? If you don't have a unique product or service offer then you compete on price and convenience: who has the best price, and who is closest to the customer? Yet if you have uniqueness, a point of difference over your competition, then consumers will be attracted to your product and services. If you don't have uniqueness, then you need some way of keeping your customers. Our customer retention strategy is a VIP Loyalty Club.

Knowing our market (customer), and what business we are in, enables us to differentiate ourselves from our competitors and build our brand on trust and recognition. We underpin these values with product offers that are supported by our VIP Loyalty Club. Targeting our customers with unique service and product values, backed up with a rewards strategy, is the glue that cements customer loyalty. This in turn builds valuable referral business. If you are still wondering what uniqueness you can apply to your business then think about the one obvious experience we all want and rarely get: excellent customer service.

The super brands

I have learned that travel is 'the university of life', and nothing gives me greater satisfaction than to attend the classrooms of the world's best brand builders. Over the past decade I have been going on campus most years and, accordingly, include a travel budget in our annual business plan. I do it for two important reasons. Much needed R and R and self-education. I am always fascinated to observe the importance of brand power. Having joined several Westfield study tours in recent years I have done my share of travelling to the US – the home of the super brands. Because my family work with me in our business, each time I have taken one of them with me to help with their own education and preparation for their future.

The early nineties brought into sharp focus two distinctive retailing developments that gave consumers a clear choice between range and specialisation on the one hand and price and convenience on the other. Both were shopping experiences targeting different consumers and both coexisted because of the power of their branding statements. The big box megastore power retailers who had range, low prices and limited service, monopolised a disproportionate share of the market. The specialty retailers providing convenient locations (such as shopping malls), targeted lifestyle merchandise. They marketed their niche as relevant, exclusive, stylish, and packaged it in a recognisable brand, and they dominated the youth to baby-boomers market, all of whom had plenty of disposable income.

These two tiers of consumerism not only shaped the future of many corporations but affected world markets and heralded the arrival of the super brands. This, however, undermined tradition in retailing. The main casualties were the traditional department stores who attempted to be all things to all people, as well as, predictably, unbranded small businesses that weren't saleable but were very sinkable.

So grew the market monopolies. Brands became cultural influences like never before – the brand became an experience that was created by clever marketing. For example, sports brands were developed that consumers wanted to personally identify with; thus began huge corporate sponsorships. Driven by the mass homogenisation of new branding cultures, some products became status symbols: Levi, Calvin Klein, and Nike became fashion brands that consumers were eager to display. Starbucks became a social experience and Microsoft made IBM appear dated. While The Body Shop gave an ecological flavour to cosmetics, Virgin proved portable as it moved from music to aviation.

Meanwhile Nike and Reebok were signing star athletes to massive sponsorship deals, while at the same time commissioning third-world countries with few labour laws to manufacturer their products in the sweatshops of Asia. China in recent years has emerged as a huge source of manufactured goods for all brand merchandise. I couldn't help but notice that eighty per cent of the gifts under the tree last Christmas were manufactured in China. I am sure my family doesn't just buy on price, as many of the gifts were well-known brands. Like most consumers, however, they buy the brand and are ignorant about the place of manufacture. Hence, the power of the brand. It seems to me that many of today's brand builders are focussed on brand before product. Company's like Coke, Pepsi, Starbucks, Sony, Disney and McDonald's, however, always understood that their brands came first, therefore their brands became a way of life. When I was growing up I always remember my mum saying she was going to 'Hoover the floor'! Now that's brand power. Oddly enough, she owned an Electrolux.

Nothing, however, ignites purchasing power more than fashion brands. Some brands dwarf the product until the product is not as important as the brand and price is definitely not the purchasing mechanism. Try telling a teenager to switch from his Billabongs to a cheaper but lesser known brand.

Brand power is fuelled by marketing and change, taking the brand consistently to the market but also knowing when to change. This is where the sharp advertising agencies kick in. Look at the simplicity of Nike's 'Just do it' and Toyota's 'Oh what a feeling'. To think that a simple 'swoosh' became a global sports icon and an eight-note musical jingle propelled Toyota to market dominance. Interestingly, one of the most competitive battles in the past decade for market share dominance has been waged between Coke and Pepsi. Tag line jingles like 'The Real Thing', and 'The Pepsi Generation', have become status symbols to their brands. They are marketing statements that keep their products relevant to a youth demographic that is fickle, fad fastidious and constantly on the move. The continual process of redefining your customer's needs is critical because nothing is forever. Most of the brands I mentioned at the beginning of this book that symbolised my youth in the fifties are now gone. Brands come and go as customer preferences and perceptions change. Redefining the brand so that it matches a consumer on the move is the challenge for all market makers. Brand management is ensuring that your brand is relevant in your customers' minds when they choose to shop for your product category.

Electronic interiors

An example of redefining an established brand to match changing times is the way in which we approached our entry into the premium home cinema business. We realised that while our traditional brand, Toombul Music, had outstanding local recognition for recorded music products (CD and

DVD), the future growth in the entertainment industry wasn't music, it was consumer electronics. We needed to change. We recognised that the home of the future would incorporate computer-driven entertainment centres of almost unlimited possibilities providing us with an exciting new growth opportunity. Research showed that we needed a fresh name for our new division because we were targeting a new and different customer. And so Electronic Interiors became a division of Toombul Music. By leveraging off our core brand we not only hedged against new technology affecting our music business (downloading), but built a new business by seizing the opportunity that similar new technology provided. Our new brand is in touch with the times but is supported by a well-established business that our new clientele recognise.

BE VIS-A-BULL

How then, do small businesses survive in this greedy corporate quest for market share? Simple. Don't try to be bigger for the sake of growth, but be the best for the sake of relevance. Small business plays a vital role in today's economy and always will. Traditions change, however, and we need to adapt to market shifts and consumer preferences, to find a niche, then dominate. You need to take out the best ideas that corporate business has to offer and apply them to your business so *you* become the brand.

How do you become a brand? What are you famous for?

Marketing is one way to build brand recognition. There needs to be consistency in advertising, merchandising, promotion, publicity, loyalty club, data-base marketing, staff uniforms and web sites, all of which are significant deposits to the brand bank.

Successful brand marketers *own* their own market segment. They *become* the brand! They become famous for their market niche. Walt Disney became the brand that enchanted the children of the world. Observe what Sir Richard Branson has done with the Virgin brand, and Dick Smith did with electronics. RM Williams is globally known for his Aussie outback gear, and Steve Irwin became *The Crocodile Hunter*. Each of these business barons understood the power of personalising their brands.

How do you become a brand? What are you famous for?

Having a name like Bull was a burden to me as a youngster, but over time my name became my marketing trademark. It's quite obvious to anyone who navigates my web site, reads my books or attends my speaking presentations, that my name is my best asset and is the central focus of my marketing. It's the main attraction. It's an easily recognised symbol of my business. It's my unique selling proposition. Yet as unique as it seems, it's attention-getting in its simplicity. It took many years to build Toombul Music and by leveraging off a host brand to build another, each shared a balanced relationship, because both brands were synonymous with me.

I claim ownership of the perception of *The Music Man*. And we all know that perception is reality. Who knows, I might just become famous, but if I don't tell 'em , nobody else will! I am the ambassador of my brand and when people think of music, hopefully they will think of *The Music Man* … first!

Sir Richard Branson once said: 'If you want to be noticed, always be photographed with someone better known than yourself.' I took his advice, and over the years have been photographed with each of the many celebrities that we have presented at Toombul. After all, they are the creators of the product we sell. To be associated with the hit makers was a clear way to gain credibility over the competition and draw media attention to the business.

It really is not difficult to own your own market, to become well known for your product and services and to gain media promotion and attention if you are passionate and knowledgeable about your industry – it's being better at what you do than anyone else and letting everyone know. I also discovered that many promotion opportunities can be *free*! And everything is *promote-a-bull*.

BULLET POINTS

- Brand positioning is the impression that's made in the mind of the customer that differentiates you from the competition.

- Leverage off core competencies to build new business.

- If you want to be noticed, always be photographed with someone famous.

- Successful brand marketers *own* their own market segment. They *become* the brand.

- It's being better at what you do than anyone else and letting every one know.

Chapter 8
Publicity is free advertising

~~~~~~

BULLISM™: PROMOTE-A-BULL

Tell them quick. Tell them often.

William Wrigley Jr

n 1970 Ray Stevens had a number one song, 'Everything is beautiful, in its own way.' It was a big hit and you may remember it. I have a big business hit with a similar lyric ... *Everything is promote-a-bull, in its own way!*

I previously alluded to *free* media exposure. Let me share with you some ways to *outsmart – not outspend*.

Smaller businesses have smaller marketing budgets and cannot compete with the muscle of the mass marketers. They cannot outspend their competition but need to find ways to outsmart their business rivals. It's really easy. I get a kick out of getting publicity because it's free advertising. Mind you, having a secret weapon like *No is Negotiable* certainly helps. When someone says 'No' to me, 'it's like a red rag to a Bull' and my response is always: 'What the heck – what have I got to lose?'

I take 'the Bull by the horns' and go back fighting. Over the years, we built a business with a significant profile without spending much money on marketing. I convinced my suppliers that it was worthwhile for them to provide strong advertising support and I got to know key media who saw value in telling our story about our celebrity appearances.

Our business gained high exposure because of the association it's had with the music legends who have participated in promotions with us over the years. It's a unique marketing tactic that gave us national recognition.

For almost twenty-five years Toombul Music has presented more superstars and celebrities on the centre stage of a shopping centre than any other Australian retailer. While this became our claim to fame, it also became our point of difference. This single activity lifted us out of the normal competitive mainstream and set us apart from others. We gained extraordinary customer loyalty by providing an unforgettable experience for our customers and, at the same time, brought matchless value and reputation to our business.

Since formulating the simple idea of presenting artists on the centre stage at Toombul, way back in 1981, this activity has brought significant publicity and media attention to our business. Once our reputation was established for organising highly effective presentations and performances by music celebrities, record companies seized the opportunity to encourage their artists to perform with us, because it sold a lot of product. Because we are an ARIA survey chart store, it also provided a healthy weekly chart position for the artist. So the artists performed for free to promote their latest offering. The shopping centre marketed the event, as it attracted significant customer traffic to their centre which benefited other retailers. And our customers loved it.

It was a win-win for everybody. There were tangible benefits for everyone and the best promotion campaigns are when everyone wins.

This single activity ignited countless publicity opportunities due to the public's insatiable thirst for celebrity. I always seized the opportunity to interview the artists on stage in order to control the event. Predictably, I was on TV or in the paper the next day with a celebrity entertainer. When Sir Richard Branson said: 'If you want to be noticed always be photographed with someone famous' – he wasn't kidding! It's powerful advice!

By beginning with a *good* idea, we became *better* each time we presented a celebrity and by learning from mistakes and measuring our performance we became arguably the *best* in the country at celebrity 'event marketing'. We were one of the first music retailers in the country to develop these full-scale marketing events. Here are a few more *firsts*.

When The Corrs appeared for us at Toombul in 1997 on their promotion tour of their first album, their impromptu performance was the first time they had played to an Australian audience.

John Denver told me once that he had never done a shopping centre promotion before.

Michael Crawford informed me that he had never been interviewed by a retailer before.

Sir Cliff Richard said that his numerous appearances with us had become a tradition, but they were the only retail appearance in the world that he continually does.

It didn't stop there, however. All this activity started to get us noticed by Westfield who, under our lease conditions, monitored our sales results. So we began to win some serious national awards. Eventually we were awarded more than any other retailer in Westfield's Australasian portfolio. Each time we won an award we benefited from the national publicity that Westfield generated, so we kept attempting to win more. We were on a roll and the publicity was very generous.

An award is a gift of encouragement.

Al Pacino

I don't know about you, but my career highlights have always been the times when I achieved something for the very *first* time. I suppose this is because of the realisation that a dream has become reality and a goal has been achieved. Like when I first learned how to stay on my Malvern Star push bike without falling off! A bloody sore backside is a good teacher. Learning to play my first song on my five pound guitar was my *first* musical milestone.

And the winner is ...

I vividly recall the evening when we won our very *first* Westfield National Award in 1992. It took ten years to win that terrific trophy! After years of developing my *Hit List*, which became the structure for *The Bullseye Principle*, I was eventually on the centre stage of the palatial Sydney Regent Hotel's grand ballroom, to claim a prize that I'd worked so long to achieve.

My brief acceptance speech to my peers in the audience was ... 'I'd like to thank Westfield for helping me achieve my dream, my goal ... *not to be the biggest ... but to be the best* ... music retailer in Australia!'

I received a standing ovation! I'm not sure if it was because it was a difficult award to win ... or because my speech was short! All night long I'd been listening to award winners thank everyone in their organisation from the van driver to the CEO.

There's a fine line between winners and wallies!

This win was a 'gift of encouragement', and in the next four years we won the award three times, a first for the awards program. In 1997 our business was an inaugural inductee into the Westfield Hall of Fame, and in 2001, Westfield presented me with a 'Westfield Legend Award'. At the time I thought, *Wow! This is as good as it gets*, but it wasn't. A personal career highlight occurred in 2003 when I was honoured with a Commonwealth Centenary Medal for distinguished achievements in business by the Australian Government.

While all this was happening, however, I was having fun. Stretching my limits, pushing the bar higher, focussing on achieving goals, hitting targets and going out on a limb for a cause I really believe in.

Starting AMRA (Australian Music Retailers Association) back in 1992 was such a cause. The record companies were losing the fight against deregulation with the ACCC (Australian Competition and Consumer Commission). The record companies had ARIA (Australian Record Industry Association), a well-funded industry body, to lobby and liaise with government. Retailers had no representative body and due to the arrogance of the record companies over CD prices the fate of retailers was not within their own control.

With the support of a few independent retail buddies, I became the first chairman of AMRA, a role I filled for the next five years. We quickly united the retail fraternity into a representative body to talk to government. Suddenly I was in Canberra speaking to government ministers, on a mission to protect the rights of retailers. Sadly we lost the battle and the government introduced parallel importing of music which allowed music to be imported instead of being controlled by the local record industry.

The fortunes of the music industry changed with that piece of legislation. Prices were forced down because of the public perception that CDs were too expensive and they never returned. The body and soul of the industry was also devalued.

We got on with building the Association regardless, and united the industry with two national music conferences that showcased the music industry and united all participants. It was at this point that I became a national spokesperson for the retail music industry and our business was exposed to the national media.

AMRA has progressed into an essential platform to integrate retail issues with ARIA and government, such as effective industry compliance to sensitive consumer protection issues. The true value of an industry association is to strengthen the entire distribution chain and to create dialogue between governments and industry to benefit all participants. AMRA was another first.

Marketing without money

When was the last time that your customers read about you in the press, heard you on the radio or saw you on TV? You're good at what you do and nobody has goods or services as good as yours, right? Then how do you communicate this to your customers and prospective clients? If you're really serious about building your business then you need to get real serious about getting yourself noticed by the media. Finding opportunities to get free media coverage for you and your business is not difficult. You just need to know how to go about it.

My formula for successful marketing is the timely connection of the product with the advertising, merchandising, promotion and publicity. While it's easy to understand the value of the first three elements, the value of publicity is misunderstood by many merchants when it comes to cost-effective marketing. Publicity is a credible component in building your brand and adding valuable goodwill to your business. Regular public-relations campaigns, however, can be expensive if you employ a publicist, yet there are simple ways to gain media attention that cost nothing. Paradoxically, the publicity that you don't pay for can be more effective and credible than the advertising that you do pay for. What the media say about you often has a more significant impact on your business because people understand that advertising is prepared and paid for, whereas information reported by a neutral third party is more likely to be unbiased or 'true'.

PR is a specialised skill and for best results you should employ a good publicist, so you can focus on what you do best. If this is not an option, then let me show you some tactics for getting free media coverage.

Let's apply *The Bullseye Principle.*

1. Set your sights

Focus on what product or event or opportunity it is that you want to publicise and work out what you want to achieve.

2. Plan the process

Commit to building your media plan (publicity) into your business plan, which means regularly informing media about your products or services. What is the timing? How will this event be integrated into the overall marketing plan (for example, with promotion and advertising)?

Begin to compile a media data base that deals with your market area. Read local papers and magazines to target those journalists who are writing about topics that influence your industry and are relevant to your business. The catering industry does this well by smooching to restaurant and food reviewers. By reading reviewers' columns, it's easy to find email addresses.

Email is the best and cheapest form of communicating your message. Confine your message to a concise *one page* document and *don't* email attachments – they won't be opened. Personalise your communication so your story is read by the right person.

3. Implement the strategy

Write a media release. What is your message? What do you want to say and to whom? Select topics that will be of interest to the community, such as a special event, or by presenting an 'idol' pop star, or a well-known author, a celebrity, or people in your industry who are known and respected. An exciting and innovative new product release or winning an industry award is a great reason to blow your own trumpet. Each time our business won an industry award we issued a media release on our achievement; it was an opportunity to draw attention to our business. As the awards increased, so did the media attention. We would announce an award win with headlines such as: 'Not the biggest but the best', or 'Music biz tops the chart'.

Always have a compelling headline to your media release to gain attention. Most journalists receive so much information that they scan the headlines looking for interesting stories, and as we all know, headlines sell. Browse through any newspaper or magazine to see the importance that an editor places on headlines. Keep them short and creative so your release stands out from all the rest and encourages the recipient to read on, just as a headline in a newspaper or magazine commands your attention. When our business won the Westfield National Independent Specialty Retailer Award for the third time, our media release read: 'Music retailer takes the hat trick!'

When we promoted Tommy Emmanuel's appearance the headline read: 'Tommy at Toombul.' When Harry Connick Jr came, the release said: 'When Harry met Barry!' Get the idea? The purpose here was to grab media attention for our event so they could write about the occasion, or speak about it on radio or feature the promotion on TV. Short, punchy, attention-grabbing headlines made our message stand out.

Predictably, all our superstar presentations – The Corrs, Cliff Richard, Michael Crawford, John Farnham, Olivia and Slim – were featured on the

Always have a compelling headline on your press release to gain attention.

six o'clock news. And my customers would call me the next day to tell me they saw me on the 'telly' and I would quietly thank Richard Branson for the great idea that I picked up from his autobiography.

When my first book *A Little Bull Goes a Long Way* was released, I knew that the title was cheeky enough to create a second look. One week after I issued my media release, Channel Nine's 'Brisbane Extra' did a feature story on my life and business. Their interest in the story was that a local retailer had become an author, and we benefited greatly from the state-wide television coverage.

I sent a media release to the Queensland Premier's Department and asked if he would officially launch my new book. He agreed. Premier Beattie has always been a supporter of Queensland small business and a great advocate of local entrepreneurship. To make this a big event I proposed to the Department of State Development that I present a free business seminar and all royalties from my book sold at the launch would be donated to the Northside Chamber of Commerce. They strongly marketed the event to people on their considerable data base and six hundred turned up at the Kedron Wavell Services Club to hear the premier introduce my business presentation and launch my book.

One month later Richard Wilkins invited me to appear on Channel Nine's 'The Today Show', and a national television audience got 'a little Bull' for breakfast! Richard introduced me as 'a legend in the music industry' and referred to me as *The Music Man*. Where did he get his information from? You guessed it, my media release, which contained my biography and web site address.

Have you got a biography? If you want to be well known in the community, then you had better get one. If you have difficulty, then ask a publicist to write one for you. Importantly, place your biography and media releases on your web site and be sure to list your web site address on your media releases. This way people have easy access to a more detailed description of your business. The internet can be a most useful and cost-effective information source and sometimes all it takes is a compelling media release to turn it into a powerful promotion tool.

Once you establish a worthy media list, it's important to put yourself on *their* list. I continually receive calls from the media when they are doing research on topics that relate to the music industry.

Brisbane's top talk-back radio station 4BC invited me to be a guest on their evening chat show. This developed into a regular weekly segment and every Monday night, the host discusses new music releases with *The Music Man*.

It's all about profile – building your image – getting your face out there and telling your community your story. Let them know you are the best. Once you build a profile you have a good chance that your customer will think of you first and this is the first step in dominating your market category.

The best real estate consultants that I know are the award winners who tell their community they are their industry's top achievers. This attracts sellers to list their properties with them and gives buyers confidence that they are dealing with an experienced professional. Everyone loves a winner and nobody likes to win more than real estate consultants. I should know, I have bought and sold a few houses in my time and speak to lots of them. In fact just recently I was speaking to hundreds of them!

I was presenting at a large national real estate conference in Perth and when I came off the stage several delegates asked to be photographed with me. This occurs regularly after I explain to my audience the success I have had from Richard Branson's 'photo opportunity' idea. One attentive delegate showed me a proposed media release headline to accompany the photo she had just had taken with me. It read: 'Top agency meets top retailer!' She got the idea. It's amazing how one small idea can make such a big difference. But the real value of an idea lies in the using of it.

4. Deal with the issues

Sometimes your messages or objectives get lost or are unimportant to a producer of a radio or TV program or an editor or journalist of a newspaper. Obviously your priorities are not theirs. This is where *No is Negotiable* works for me. Never give up. Look for another strategy. Solve the problems and find a way. Here is a story that explains how I achieved an objective by not accepting *No* for an answer: another case of persistence overcoming resistance.

In 2003, Kayleen and I moved to Queensland's Sunshine Coast to enjoy a lifestyle we feel is well earned after two decades of retailing in Brisbane. Another reason was to distance ourselves a little from our business so that our family could assume management roles and I could concentrate on developing my speaking career. I also had ideas for another book. I was struggling, however, to find the time and the motivation to accumulate content to write a sequel to *A Little Bull*, which by that time had become a good seller.

My motivation came in a most unusual way. And as it turned out, I achieved two goals at the same time!

I decided to promote my own business seminar in the region to assist small business and to introduce myself to the local business community as a speaker and business coach. The Queensland Government State Development and Innovation Centre agreed to sponsor my seminar and I needed a major local newspaper to promote the event. I approached the region's largest newspaper, *The Sunshine Coast Daily*, for their support. When I telephoned their promotions manager, however, I received a polite but firm 'No' to my sponsorship proposal. I had an idea.

I asked if I could speak to the editor-in-chief as I assumed that he was the real decision-maker – the corporate structure of the publishing industry differs from that of traditional business in one significant way – the editor has overriding control of what is published, not the general manager or up-line management.

I was also careful to explain to the promotions manager that I was discussing another editorial matter, so as not to compromise our relationship. You need to be sensitive so that you don't offend contacts as you climb the corporate ladder to reach the decision-maker. Once the decision is made the task is usually carried out by subordinates.

My objective was to write a regular business column in a local newspaper to build my profile within the community and at the same time discipline myself to develop content for my new book. (Discipline is a major factor in achieving goals.)

As it turned out, Peter Owen, the editor-in-chief, is a very experienced executive and a beaut bloke. He reacted positively to my proposal. He liked the idea because he was planning on increasing the content in the business section of the paper and my call was timely. We all know that timing is everything, and I sensed my timing was right to turn the negative I had just received from the promotion manager into a positive.

So I asked the predictable question, hoping he knew who I was. I said: 'Now that I am going to become a regular business writer for you ... wouldn't it be a good idea for the paper to promote my forthcoming business seminar?' There was dead silence for a moment and I thought ... bugger ... have I gone too far this time?

Suddenly I heard laughter on the other end of the phone and Peter cheerfully replied: 'Of course I know who you are, Barry, I've read your book! And *you* are doing *No is Negotiable* – on me!'

'It really works, don't you think?' I said, tongue in cheek.

'It sure worked on me!' he cheerfully replied.

Peter readily agreed to promote my seminar, because now there was value to the newspaper in building my profile. It was a win-win, which is the key ingredient in my negotiation recipe.

It was the beginning of a worthwhile partnership and 'Barry's Bullisms' became a weekly business feature in *The Sunshine Coast Daily*. It also got me started on the book you are now reading. I had achieved two goals at the same time; I had hit the Bullseye twice. Just like Robin Hood!

Everyone knows the legend of Robin Hood. He was an outlaw yet a champion of the people, who robbed from the rich to give to the poor. Robin was a master with a longbow, a skill for which he is traditionally celebrated. The legend says that he not only could hit the Bullseye of the target every time, but he could even split his first arrow with a second. Hollywood has made us all familiar with this feat of unerring accuracy.

My *Bullseye Principle* provides a powerful lesson in focussing, planning, and determination to hit my target (sometimes *twice* at the same time). It's an exercise in the clear-sighted aim of the spirit to win.

5. Measure performance

Be good, be better, be best. Once you get to this stage of your PR campaign, the task is to monitor the effectiveness of your performance to get the best results. You start out getting *good* secondary media, like local suburban papers to publicise your events. Once you get *better* at coming up with unique ways to draw attention to your business you will start to get the *best* coverage, such as the major daily or weekend papers with substantial circulation.

It's one thing to talk about the process, it's another to show the results. As Cuba Gooding Jr said to Tom Cruise in the hit movie, *Eddie McGuire* ... 'Show me the money!'

6. Be disciplined and determined

Be committed and focussed on your goals. Here is an example of how determination gets results.

The cover story

When I first arrived on the Sunshine Coast I noticed a well-presented weekly lifestyle magazine called *The Weekender* in my mailbox. Lisa Curry-Kenny, a well-known Olympian who lives at the coast, was on the front cover. I was impressed with its presentation so I sent the editor my biography and book. I was hoping that they would do a story on me, considering I was now a local resident. My motive was to raise my profile in the region as a business speaker and to promote my book.

I received a positive response and within a couple of weeks a journalist and photographer came to my home to do the story and take some photos. The journalist by now had read my book and studied my biography so the interview was easy. I then dropped the bombshell and asked if I could have a cover story. What better way to make an impact than to have my photo on the front cover! A bit cheeky, but why not?

The young journalist explained nicely that the decision was not hers, but it was extremely unlikely. The seed was sown, however, so I decided to persist. I said, 'Why not? You featured Lisa Curry-Kenny on the cover recently.' Now Lisa is much more attractive than I am and I could see what the polite journo was thinking. I also could see that I needed an interesting photo to do the job. Just then the photographer spotted my guitar leaning in the corner. When he asked me if I played, he gave me an idea. I said, 'Yes, I play a little.'

He replied, 'How about a song?'

'OK, as long as you put me on the *front cover*!' I said boldly. We all had a laugh but I detected that the idea of a cover story was now being considered. As I played, the photographer clicked madly. I reckon he was working at getting that cover shot and he had no argument from me.

One week later in the next issue, there I was, guitar in hand, on the front cover of *The Weekender*! Inside was a double-page feature story that headlined: *The Music Man – the cover story*. Why wasn't I surprised?

7. Hitting the Bullseye

These tactics have worked for me time and again, year in year out. Here are some of the results. Below are headlines from major newspaper and magazine articles and feature stories achieved over a twenty-two-month period.

'The Music Man' – *The Weekender*, May 2003

'Loads of sheer bull' – *Brisbane Courier Mail*, October 2003

'Barry's hit parade' – *Dynamic Small Business Magazine*, November 2003

'Barry takes the bull by the horns' – *Northern News*, Brisbane, November 2003

'He's a one man brand' – *Brisbane Courier Mail*, January 2004

'Music to the maestro' – *Brisbane Courier Mail*, January 2004

'Living for music' – *Revive Weekend Magazine, Sunshine Coast Daily*, January 2004

'No is Negotiable' – *Wealth Creator Magazine,* June 2004

'No b******t !' *Queensland Business Review,* September 2004

The examples above demonstrate how to market without money and how money can't buy good publicity. A continual well-orchestrated publicity plan can add huge awareness and credibility to your business and it's very afford-a-bull!

In January 2004, we reached over 1 000 000 people with publicity articles and features written mainly about my various business activities. That's powerful stuff when you don't have to pay for it. However, you need to provide interesting content that the media will write about. Notice that most of the headlines above are linked to my name or associated brands which have been developed and are synonymous with our business or music. What triggered these headlines? You guessed it – our media releases!

I hope now you can see the difference between advertising, promotion and publicity, and why it's important that they all work together in harmony. Whilst all support each other, a good promotion plan provides ongoing public awareness of your business. The real value, however, is business and personal brand development.

Everything is *promote-a-bull*, in its own way!

BULLET POINTS

- The best promotion campaigns are when everyone wins.

- A win, like an award, is a gift of encouragement.

- Successful marketing is the timely connection of product with advertising, merchandising, promotion and publicity.

- Compile a media list, write a media release, include your biography.

- Determination is the clear-sighted aim of the spirit to win.

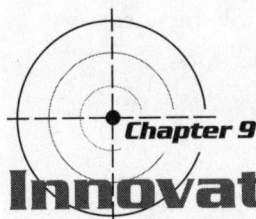

Chapter 9

Innovate don't imitate

BULLISM:™ CREATE-A-BULL

Create, don't compete – innovate, don't imitate.

Barry Bull

D on't study your competitors' every tactic and try to copy or compete. Instead do things differently and create new business through innovation, not imitation. Don't look in the rear-vision mirror. Instead keep your lights on high beam and your eyes focussed on where you are going, not where you've been. You will see new ideas that will create new opportunities, new directions and new customers.

> *Opportunities are usually described as hard work,*
> *so most people don't recognise them.*

> Ann Landers

Every successful product was first conceived from an opportunity to produce something new and beneficial for consumers. Every successful business was born out of an opportunity to create something different. The trick is to know what the market wants or is ready for, and to get there before your competition catches on. Alert business entrepreneurs are innovators always looking for that opportunity to be different.

A creative person's greatest asset is to recognise potential and opportunity which is not immediately apparent to others. Successful businesses are built by using innovative techniques to create a reproducible business system and finding creative ways to differentiate from competitors.

What is your point of difference? What are you famous for? What keeps your customers coming back?

For me it is always looking for that creative edge and trying to push the boundary of opportunity as far as possible. Years ago we hit on the idea of presenting celebrities on the centre stage of a shopping centre. We developed an untried idea into an enormous promotional opportunity that was also difficult for our competition to copy. We became the connector between the people who make the music and those who buy it. I call it *taking the dream makers to the dream takers*, which simply means presenting well-known entertainers, who originated a piece of musical artistry, to people who enjoyed and became captivated by their talent. This single activity lifted our business out of the competitive mainstream of our industry and ignited explosive customer contact. This led to opportunities to establish our own VIP Loyalty Club. We developed useful data base customer capture programs by inviting all our customers to join our club. This enabled us to segment their musical tastes and target their specific interests. Profiling customer needs has always been the core focus of successful marketers; finding the right customer who wants your product or service and tailoring your offer to suit them. While this was happening we gained exceptional customer loyalty by providing an unforgettable experience with our celebrity promotions. This single example of differentiation brought considerable profile to our business.

Differentiation

Differentiation is to know how to distinguish your business, in the minds of your customers, from other businesses. You add value and provide your customers with a reason why they should choose your product or services over others. Differentiation allows you to stand tall from your competition. If you don't give your customer a reason to buy from you, they won't. If you can continually give to them good reasons and they do, this is the cheapest form of advertising.

Fact file: The old retail rules says that it costs six times as much to gain a new customer as it takes to keep existing ones.

Over sixty per cent of our sales come from existing satisfied customers. Repeat purchases and referral business is fundamental to our core sales procedures. You never close a sale, you open a long-term relationship. Every time our customers return to our store our relationship with them grows, and by understanding and catering to their needs we sponsor trust, loyalty and referral business. This is why our VIP Loyalty Club is important. We target our customers' interests and reward them for their loyalty.

Here's how it works. We offer our regular customers a compelling reason to join our VIP Loyalty Club with free membership. We call it VIP because we want our customers to know they are *very important people* to our business. We ask them to complete an application form which provides us with their details: age, address, email, age of children, concerts they attend and, importantly, their favourite artists. We issue them an official club membership card and each time they buy from us their purchases accrue points, just like the airlines do with their frequent-flyer programs. When their points balance reaches a threshold they are offered rewards off their next purchase.

It's called customer care. You can get an insurance policy for most things in business – theft, fire, flood, public liability – but you can't get an insurance policy to protect the business's most important asset – your customers. *Our VIP Club is our insurance policy against customer loss.* It also allows us to invite them to special events, give them access to exclusive autographed product and a chance to meet their favourite celebrity. All of these offers are targeted towards our VIP members.

The reason for this is simple: it is to make them feel special, to give them a reason to belong to our club and to reward them accordingly. That's why it's called a loyalty club. *You must give loyalty if you expect to get it in return.*

Whilst technology enables all of this, it must be remembered that the interface with the customer is critical. If the point of contact between you and your customer is not a pleasurable experience then all the technology in the world won't get your customer relationship past the first contact.

Here are the five key steps we used to set up our VIP Club.

1. **Develop an application procedure and loyalty customer card**. The first step is to obtain your customer profile (with their permission) and begin building your data base. Print a loyalty card that contains a bar code that facilitates customer identification.

2. **Obtain a software program that enables customer capture details**. Apart from contact information (email and residential addresses) you need to be able to track customer purchases to analyse their buying patterns: the type of merchandise (size, style, genre, artist, author, etc.) what their purchasing habits are, who the biggest spenders are.

3. **Easy interface with point of sale**. It needs to have an easy link at the point of purchase. In our case the customer presents their club card and the barcode is scanned and linked to their purchases.

4. **Reward benefits – a win-win**. In order to obtain the information required to effectively target client needs, you must reward them with benefits. By allocating points on the value of each transaction, they are then translated into value for the customer once a predetermined threshold is attained.

5. **Target marketing**. The purpose of all of this is to gather information that is valuable in targeting your clientele. By attaching each sale to a specific customer enables you to target their interests and introduce new merchandise or services to a customer you now know.

Targeting a customer you know

Instead of allocating our total advertising budget to traditional campaigns, the success of which can't be easily measured, we devote considerable energy to our club marketing, because those efforts and results *are* measurable.

We've all heard of the eighty/twenty rule where eighty per cent of sales come from twenty per cent of customers. Accordingly, eighty per cent of the profit comes from those same twenty per cent of customers. With traditional advertising, it is so easy to spend eighty per cent of your ad budget on the wrong twenty per cent of your customers. You're not spending money trying to get your loyal customers to spend more, instead you're wasting money trying to convert consumers who have no interest in your offer. The science here is to target your loyal customers. Smaller businesses do not have deep pockets and cannot waste hard-earned profits. This is where a targeted customer approach works because we are targeting a good customer who knows us and whom we know.

By targeting our data base with certain product offers, we can be confident that results will be more effective because we are target marketing to a customer we know. Understanding their purchasing habits tells us which products they buy. This is why we ask the ages of other family members, because music has a broad demographic and appeals to all members of the family. The next step is to market events that target an identified demographic.

Event marketing

Whenever we invite The Wiggles to the store for a new product promotion, we target the five-year-old demographic. These are the children of our club members. When those kids find out that The Wiggles are coming to Toombul, all hell breaks loose in the household until their parents agree to take them to our event. Of all the celebrities we have presented over the years, who do you think attracted the biggest audiences? Cliff, The Corrs, Slim, Ronan, Barnsey or Farnsey? No. You got it – The Wiggles!

The last time they came, Anthony (Wiggle) was absent so I put on his blue T-shirt and introduced the boys to the stage. I did the 'hot potato' with them … and 2000 kids wanted *my autograph!*

We do three catalogue direct-mail campaigns a year to an active data base of several thousand. We provide dozens of exclusive special product offers (like personally autographed product) that are not available anywhere else and are offered first to our club members. While this is very effective it is also time consuming and expensive for a single store. It does, however, allow us to maintain and cleanse the data base by eliminating 'return to sender' rejects that have been returned because of customers who have changed their address.

Email marketing is the better method. It is a faster, more cost-effective way to communicate with our customers and gets results that traditional advertising cannot achieve.

Once you have your email data base it's very affordable to maintain and use. Here are a few simple tips to effective email marketing:

- Always seek your customer's approval for their details and permission to communicate information by email.

- Keep your message short and to the point.

- Use good, concise headline statements.

- Definitely *no* attachments; they can contain viruses and people don't open them.

- Use colour as a highlight, not as a format. Whilst colour fonts look great they also increase the size of the download and can be slow if broadband is not connected.

- Use the KISS principle, *Keep It Simple, Silly.*

And, speaking of KISS ... here's an example of effective email marketing.

In May 2004 Gene Simmons was in Australia promoting his new solo album. For those who missed the seventies, there were two bands that captivated the world during that decade: Abba and Kiss. Gene Simmons was the fire-breathing, blood-spitting, rubber-tongue, bass guitarist of Kiss. Love 'em or hate 'em, they sang an anthem to a generation of fans and they still have a huge obsessive fan base today. Known as the 'Kiss Army', several hundred belong to our VIP Club.

Because of this, Toombul Music was one of the only stores in the country where Gene agreed to meet his fans and to personally autograph his new CD. To meet a real rock icon is a big deal for any music fans. And, as we expected, we had some difficulties. We were not permitted to promote the event until Gene had completed his obligation with his main sponsor, just in case our event compromised his reason for being in the country. We had just *one day* to promote the store appearance because he was due to leave Brisbane the very next day. There was no time to organise effective press or radio. We were in a dilemma as to how we could effectively market the event in just twenty-four hours.

Our VIP Club data base was the perfect solution. We emailed our Kiss fans and invited them to a special event to meet the man himself, to get his new CD personally autographed, and to tell their friends. After all, word of mouth is the cheapest and most credible form of advertising. And did the 'Kiss Army' react! The next day was mayhem! Hundreds were lined up outside our store and the phone was ringing like a fire alarm. The queue went through the store, down the malls, into the car park, and headed towards the airport! We sold hundreds of pieces of product that day and our customers loved the experience. Gene was fairly chuffed too!

Incidentally, over their illustrious thirty-year career, Kiss have sold 80 000 000 albums.

Creativity is looking at what everyone else is looking at and seeing something different!

It's the products we sell that provide the opportunity to creatively market a different offer. I hear small business operators complain every day about the mass marketers monopolising new product opportunities with predatory pricing. At the risk of repeating myself (because this message is worth repeating), if you are in specialty business, there is no value in just selling the same product as the mass marketers – because price becomes the issue. Who's the cheapest, and who's closest to the customer? Finding ways to add value to a *different* product, delivers sales with healthy profit.

Importantly, it's knowing what your customer wants!

Not all customers are the same – they all have different tastes and prefer-ences. Our record company suppliers release hundreds of new products every month in all types of genres that appeal to a broad range of music lovers. To emphasise my point about *the product* being the opportunity to

Creativity is looking at what everyone else is looking at and seeing something different!

creatively market a different offer, the following examples explain how we efficiently use our VIP Club to target a customer who becomes *ours* – exclusively.

We assess the hundreds of new products available to us each week and seek out the hidden gems that the mass marketers may miss or won't predictably exploit. We then determine the product's potential through creative merchandising and promotion. Finally we market to a customer we know wants something different.

The key is to know what our customers want.

Bachelor boy

In early December 2004 Cliff Richard released his first new studio album in three years. We have over 500 Cliff fans on our data base and they are all aware that Toombul Music is the *only* retailer he agrees to visit when he is touring Australia.

On this occasion, we invited his Brisbane fans to an exclusive after-hours cocktail party at our store to celebrate the release of his new album. We entertained them with his latest DVD concert on a wide-screen plasma TV, played his new album and I even got out the trusty guitar and sang them a few Cliff classics. Not exactly a 'cliffhanging' performance, as my band days have long gone; however, the fans sang along in the spirit of the occasion because this event was just for them. We made a special effort for them because they are worth it. They are our most loyal customers. I also had a *big* surprise up my sleeve which I will tell you about later.

Over the years, this activity has become a tradition. On one occasion I received a surprise video message from the man himself and the Cliff fans loved it. We became the connection to their hero, which is why they enthusiastically support these events. Predictably, they all become *our* customers. I expect that we sell more Cliff Richard and Kiss product than any other Aussie retailer because we *know* our customer and we know what *they* want. And importantly, *they* know we know, as the following testimonial from the President of Cliff's Australian fan club illustrates.

Before I became the President of the Sir Cliff Richard Movement of
Australia I thought Toombul Music was 'just another music store.'
I soon realised that Barry's passion for music infects those around
him; he and his wonderful staff are totally committed to satisfying
the individual as well as the organisation or fan club, and that is
the driving force behind his business. With satisfaction guaranteed;
wouldn't *you* keep going back?

Joanne Saunders
CRMA Melbourne

We organise these special events for Kiss, Cliff, Elvis, Farnham and even
Jimmy Buffet fans. 'Jimmy who?' you ask.

Margaritaville and Parrotheads

Jimmy Buffet rose to fame in the seventies with an easygoing, tropical
folk–rock sound that reflected the lifestyle of a beach bum character that
has endeared him to millions. A kind of 'don't worry, be happy' musical
legacy with a style that borders on 'The Eagles with a sea breeze!' Wherever
you find an endless summer or a margarita cocktail you will find a Jimmy
Buffet fan. He calls them 'parrotheads' and they have turned his concerts
into Mardi Gras. Jimmy is a smart businessman who has leveraged off a
successful recording career to open a string of nightclubs called *Margari-
taville*, which was the title of a top-ten hit for him way back in 1977. He
also markets a range of exclusive tropical beach apparel – something every
beach bum needs.

While Jimmy has earned a huge following in the US with his Caribbean-style
beach music, it is not mainstream in this country. Consequently not a lot of
his CDs are available in Aussie stores.

My son Gavin, who manages our music retail division, is a big Jimmy
Buffet fan. As you might expect, we carry the entire Buffet range. Gavin
saw an opportunity to support a growing data base of Jimmy Buffet fans
by importing an exclusive range of tropical 'beach party' T-shirts that were
being marketed at Jimmy's Florida concerts. Aside from the Florida climate

being similar to Brisbane's, this coincided with a new Jimmy Buffet CD release – his best in years.

Gavin discovered that the exclusive Jimmy Buffet Aussie fan club organise an annual beach-party night attended by fans from all over the country. Their next big gathering was scheduled at Kawana on the Queensland Sunshine Coast, not far from where I live. He asked the organisers if he could attend the event and set up a sales booth to display the new merchandise. Kayleen and I went along to assist our young son's enthusiastic initiative, not knowing what to expect. It was fortuitous that we did because 400 fans arrived to hear the live music from the Jimmy Buffet cover bands and sip the margaritas! And they were ready *to party*!

The joint was jumping as they all shared the love of one man's music. And they loved our merchandise. We sold everything but the cash register! Gavin was so excited as he signed up many of the 'parrotheads' to our VIP Club and made lots of new customers that evening.

EXCITE-A-BULL

As I stood and proudly watched 'the young Bull' charge, I noticed how his excitement was contagious. Excitement is a magical human emotion that is not only transferable but is also the life blood of any business. Excitable people are valuable and are usually leaders, because they have the ability to ignite the spark of enthusiasm in others.

The three things we look for when recruiting are:

- attitude,
- energy, and
- excitement.

Bugger the report card!

Excitement is like the measles, unchecked it is highly contagious.

Specialise don't commercialise

Big opportunities exist for astute merchants who are close to their product. Exposing new product to a niche market that is ignored by mainstream merchants opens doors of exclusive potential and opportunity. If you're in a specialty business then *specialise*. There is a huge segment of the market just waiting for your specialty. *Create don't compete – innovate don't imitate.*

> *A pessimist sees the difficulty in every opportunity; an optimist sees the opportunity in every difficulty.*
>
> Winston Churchill

BULLET POINTS

- Opportunities are usually described as hard work, so most people don't recognise them.

- Never close a sale – open a long-term relationship.

- You can get an insurance policy for most things in business – theft, fire, flood, public liability – but you can't get an insurance policy to protect the business's most important asset – your customers.

- Give loyalty if you expect to get it in return.

- Creativity is looking at what everyone else is looking at and seeing something different!

- Excitement is like the measles, unchecked it's highly contagious.

- Specialise – don't commercialise.

Chapter 10

The power of people connections

BULLISM:™ CONNECT-A-BULL

What you give out always comes back in some way and at some time.

Anon.

I am an ordinary bloke who started out without money but with a passion for music and a desire to control my own destiny. Like everyone, I suffered setbacks and obstacles, but eventually adversity and disappointment led to opportunity and growth. I then discovered that failure and success were connected. You have to fall off your bike and suffer some pain before you learn to ride correctly. This was an important early lesson in my life. Learning to respect the knowledge required to accomplish the task in order to move forward. The key factor is to get back on your bike and try again.

Armed with this realisation, I began to link my successful business lessons into a sequence that I call my *Bullseye Principle*. Each time I missed my Bullseye target I would analyse where I went wrong and get back on target.

I believe everything in life is connected. While I don't believe in coincidences I react to circumstances that impose a sense of déjà vu, and a feeling of familiarity. Too many unexplained occurrences happen in life for things not to be somehow related. I am sure you know what I mean. The challenge is to unravel the puzzle to understand the connections. What goes where? Why did that happen and for what reason? A good place to start is to understand that the process exists.

I regret that I have had to live a good deal of my life to come to this realisation. Now that I am alert to this I look for the connections between events that come into my life wherever I can, and sometimes they happen in a most unexpected way. *You never know what's waiting around the next bend.*

Six months after the release of my first book my publisher proposed a concept for a second. She suggested I write a little inspirational book of all my motivational sayings (my Bullisms) that had salted and peppered *A little Bull*. I needed some time to contemplate this as I had never considered that I had any more books in me. So I shelved the project, hoping the right concept would eventually present itself.

It did – just six months later. The way it happened, however, makes an interesting tale, particularly for anyone who believes in the karma that 'things are meant to be'.

I had been speaking in Wanganui, on the west coast of New Zealand's north island, and was driving to Wellington where I was presenting at a business breakfast the next morning. I was accompanying Debbie Tawse, the principle of Celebrity Speakers (the New Zealand speaking agency that was sponsoring my presentation). On the way Deb said to me with a grin: 'There's a small town up ahead where we will stop for lunch. I think you will find it interesting.' What an understatement that turned out to be! As we turned the next bend I spotted a small sign on the highway, which I was about to discover was another signpost on the road to my destiny. The sign said 'Welcome to Bulls'. I turned to Deb and shouted, 'Bugger me — they've named a town after me!'

Bulls is a small town in New Zealand's Manawatu province, named after an early settler, James Bull. What grabbed my attention, however, was the clever way the town's tourist bureau marketed their local businesses and services. The chiropractor was called 'Fix-a-bull', the police station was labelled 'Const-a-bull', the haberdashery was 'Stitch-a-bull' and the café was branded 'Full-as-a-bull'.

So began the idea for *My Little Book of Bull*. After this, there was no stopping the potential for 'Barry's Bullisms'. Isn't it weird how things in life are linked or connected? – particularly if you are prepared to take notice and follow your intuition. Intuition is a powerful instinct – if only we'd take notice of it more often.

To add to the irony I recently called a good Kiwi friend to obtain a little more background on Bulls as I was researching this story. He took the call on his mobile and said, 'I'm in the car Barry, can you wait a moment? I'm just driving into a town where I can stop and talk to you.' I asked him where he was. To my astonishment he replied: 'I've just arrived at Bulls!'

Connecting information

I meet many people during my active business schedule and it is the power of people connection that provides the best outcomes and reward. In my dual roles as retailer and business presenter, I am fortunate to have the opportunity to network with many other capable people and share their experiences. So often the roles are reversed. A willingness to switch from teacher to student has allowed me to consider the viewpoint of others and to respect the value of shared knowledge.

I am a big believer in research and some of my most daring decisions have been as a result of good research and advice. Equally, some of my nastiest nightmares occurred through lack of the right information. Collecting the right data through research is a fundamental necessity in successful business building and not only shows strengths but identifies weaknesses. It's so easy to rush into making decisions without getting all the facts. The old saying 'If in doubt, check it out' is a handy reminder here.

It was mid-summer 2005 and I was sitting in a street-side city coffee shop waiting to see my solicitor. While being romanced by the blend of a cappuccino, I watched the sea of humanity passing my island in the humidity of this balmy Brisbane morning. Suddenly a face stood out on the crowded street as eyes connected and a vague recognition of a friendship long ago rekindled.

Peter Butler was program manager of Radio 5AD Adelaide when I was head of marketing at CBS way back in the mid-seventies. He had helped me to launch many famous careers including Meatloaf, Billy Joel and Boz Scaggs. I hadn't seen Peter in twenty-five years. As we both had scheduled appointments we exchanged business cards and agreed to reconnect. There was a distinct feeling of synchronicity, however, when he informed me that he operated his own radio and research consultancy company on the Gold Coast. As I mentioned previously, I react to serendipitous occasions like this because I believe they happen for a reason.

Two weeks later we met and discussed our careers. We discovered we had much in common and agreed to consider pursuing some opportunities that matched our combined talents. Perhaps one of the most important lessons learned in my life has been recognising opportunities to partner with other like-minded capable people. Like everything in life, however, opportunities have a habit of tip-toeing by if you let them.

I was particularly engaged in Peter's lifelong passion and understanding of the importance of research. I asked him to explain how connecting information is critical to every business decision.

> When Barry and I recently met up in Brisbane, after all those years, it led immediately to a mini research campaign. What was I doing? What was he doing? How was his wife and family? How was his business? How often did he speak at functions? Where did he speak? When was the next engagement? These were just some of the questions that whipped around the coffee shop that morning in a matter of minutes. It gave me answers to questions that I needed or wanted to know and at the same time Barry was updated on my activities with the questions he asked me.

> Everybody conducts their own research every day. Questions about health (How are you?), weekend activities (What did you do on the weekend?), football matches and scores (Did you see the game on Saturday?) are all questions that demand answers. It's that simple … and it can all be over in three questions.

Questioning leads to information and information is vital to success. It can give you the leading edge over your competitor and it can help plan the future of your business and indeed your own life.

I learned to fly a light plane (a Piper Cherokee 140) in my late teens in Sydney and one of the key factors in obtaining your instrument rating licence is 'flying blind'. The windows are covered up and your instructor is the only one who can see outside the cockpit. You then fly the aircraft with the aid of its instruments only. It's initially a difficult process for a trainee and because you don't have an outside reference to your aircraft's flying attitude— straight and level – it can cause you to lose your orientation and sense of direction. And the plane ends up in a climb or dive or turning in endless circles.

Running a business without an outside reference – finding out what your customers want – can have the same disastrous results for your business. I've seen too many companies 'crash and burn' due to a lack of market research. That's crazy, as it only needs a few 'car park questions' to get results and ensure your business is on track!

I was able to help a local optometrist increase his turnover by over 400 per cent by simply getting a clipboard and talking to 100 people in his shopping centre's car park. I asked ten questions, and it turned his entire business around. It gave him product, direction, focus and marketing knowledge that has led to his business increasing turnover from $240 000 a year to over a million dollars per annum!

My roots are in the radio industry and that industry thrives on research. It doesn't make a move without first finding out from the market what it feels and thinks. The national success of the NOVA FM network is a classic example of a research-driven product.

Research is the key to achieving your business goals and, besides, with the help of the internet, it's a fun and interesting way to find out new facts and figures.

As a result of meeting Peter Butler, I decided to 'salt and pepper' this text with researched statistical information to highlight relevant content. It's the 'seasoning that supports the reasoning'.

Connecting reality

Whilst shared knowledge is one thing, circumstance is another. Valuable knowledge is usually gained by exposure to circumstances outside your control. There is much to learn from others whose circumstances are different and sometimes the least likely teacher offers the most to learn.

Jack Johnston has been a regular of Toombul Music for over thirty years. He is one of our most loyal and long-term customers. He has a great appreciation of music and this has helped him to cope with difficult circumstances. Jack has suffered from cerebral palsy from birth and has lived his seventy plus years in a wheelchair. I remember when I first met him way back in 1981 when I first acquired our business. How could I forget him?

Whenever he came into the shop he would be smiling. After all this time, he is still the same. He knows my family well and our staff by name. He always takes an interest in their progress, and consequently, they respond accordingly. I doubt if anyone would forget him upon making his acquaintance. There is this feeling of *life* whenever Jack wheels into our store. He has always inspired me with his positive attitude and the way he copes with his disability. We have become close friends. While I assist him wherever I can, he doesn't realise how much *he* has assisted me through the years.

Not so long ago I had some difficult decisions to make, as we all do when it comes to succession planning and letting go of the reins. One Monday morning Jack arrived at the shop in a maxi taxi that accommodates his wheelchair. I hadn't seen him in a while and his eyes sparkled when he saw me. The same familiar presence that I had come to admire cheerfully illuminated the shop. He came to listen to the new Rod Stewart *American Songbook* album that I had recently featured on my 4BC radio segment. Once Jack had decided that Rod did an acceptable job on *his* favourite jazz standards, I took him to the nearby coffee shop for our traditional morning tea. I was having a bad day, however, and just feeling plain sorry for myself.

As always he asked about each of my family and was genuinely interested in their progress in the business. He remarked how fortunate I was to have such a wonderful family who shared my interests in the business and how they always looked after his needs when I was away speaking. (Jack has a most complicated entertainment system that we designed for him years ago to accommodate his needs. It has more cables than your local telecom relay station.) 'When are you going to let go, Barry?' he said, as he struggled to sip his coffee through a straw. 'Your family is ready to take the reins,' he challenged.

'You mean put the Bull out to pasture?' I replied, by this time feeling much better. He laughed out loud as he spilt his coffee. As I watched my friend (who appeared to me to need more comforting than I did) put a positive spin on my life, I considered the difficulties that *he* had to deal with *every* day. Jack certainly has a way of putting *my* life into perspective each time we meet.

Through our connection I have come to accept that things aren't always as good as they look – or as bad as they seem. Jack's connection with me, however, came through music. And it still continues. As I assisted him into the maxi taxi he said to me, 'I listen to you on the radio every Monday night and I look forward to your company. It helps me make it through the night.' Little did Jack realise how *he* had helped me make it through that day. That evening on 4BC, I played the Kris Kristofferson classic as a dedication to my friend.

Things work out best for people who make the best of the way things work out.

John Wooten

Connecting dreams

Put simply, business is an efficient way of connecting goods or services to the consumer with satisfactory mutual benefits. The efficiency in which business goes about this usually determines the quality and longevity of the business. This is one of the reasons why the casualty rate of new businesses is so high in the first five years.

I discovered early in my career that good retailing was about connections between products and customers that allow customers to differentiate

Emotion is a major motivator in purchasing.

The power of people connections

your business from all the others. The better the connection, the better the experience for the customer. When I first acquired our business I didn't have much money to promote it but I had the experience of working with celebrities. My dream was to connect the 'dream makers' with the 'dream takers' and to build a business that was very different from all the rest. I understood that my business wasn't just retailing; I had a more significant role to play. I was in the business of connecting dreams.

Developing a concept of bringing customers face to face with the music makers gave our business a differentiating edge and provided our customers with a unique and sometimes emotional experience. Emotion is a major motivator in purchasing and nothing evokes emotion quite like music. Music connects all kinds of human emotions in a way that rewards those who embrace it. It soothes the soul and is essential to the human condition.

A few years back we presented British mega-performer Michael Crawford on the centre stage to a thousand adoring fans. When presenting superstar celebrities to large audiences I find it necessary to provide a disabled area close to the stage for the elderly or incapacitated in wheelchairs, so they are not disadvantaged.

Two days before Michael was due to appear I received a call from a lady informing me that her mother was eighty-five years old, and her mum's dream was to meet Michael Crawford. I arranged for her mum to sit in the disabled area beside the stage. I asked Michael to meet all these folk personally, before the multitude of fans climbed the steps to the stage to meet him, get a photo and have their CD autographed. It was so nice to make that dear old lady's dream come true! In fact many dreams were connected that day. Including my own!

We all need dreams. If you don't have dreams how can you ever make one come true?

Over the years, I have videotaped many of the celebrities we have presented. I use them as highlights of my speaking presentations. I filmed Michael's appearance that day. The moment when he met this dear old lady is a powerful highlight in my presentations as it demonstrates the importance of the customer service experience. It is a very moving moment.

Whether it's five-year-olds at our Wiggles presentations, or fifty-year-olds meeting Sir Cliff Richard, the experience is just the same. Experience and emotion are what make our retail connection with our customers a very special component of our service offer.

And speaking of Sir Cliff, I recall at one of his early appearances (before I realised that I needed a special disabled area), I looked down from the stage and saw my friend Jack Johnston in the audience. I realised he had no hope of joining the huge queue and getting onto the stage to meet our guest celebrity. So I whispered my intention in Cliff's ear and jumped down and lifted Jack from his wheelchair and carried him to the stage to meet Cliff and be photographed. I could feel Jack's body shaking with excitement and to this day he still reminds me of the experience.

I also remind him that this little deed triggered my hernia operation, just three months later!

Nice guy!

In late 2004, we presented Australian Idol winner Guy Sebastion to 2000 loyal fans. He was at Toombul to promote his new single from his forthcoming second album. As I walked him to the stage I remarked that his new song had 'an early Michael Jackson' influence to it (*Off the Wall* is my favourite Michael Jackson outing, an album I worked back in the seventies while at CBS). Guy nodded his approval of my unbiased assessment.

As we approached the stage the 'feel' in the shopping centre erupted into an explosive roar of adulation and excitement. Guy received one of the biggest fan reactions I have ever seen in the twenty plus years of presenting celebrities. What amazed me was his appeal to every demographic; the way this charming young entertainer gave each admirer a personal moment of his time was a sign of professional maturity that went well beyond his twenty-two years.

A few weeks later the *Brisbane Courier Mail* quoted him as saying: 'As an artist there's a lot of effort that goes into being nice to everybody and effort into being the best person I can be, not only as a singer but as a role model.' Nice one, Guy! More entertainers should share your attitude.

The power of people connections

Working with artists who place high value on their customers (fans) and who understand about 'connecting dreams' is a privilege I never take for granted.

Following Guy's appearance, I spoke about the occasion and reviewed his new song on my Monday night radio segment. I gave this young entertainer a big 'thumbs up'. The next day I was surprised to learn that a transcript of my comments had been recorded and posted on the Guy Sebastion fan web site. I received dozens of emails from around the country from fans thanking me for supporting Guy. I knew then that this young entertainer was destined for bigger things. I wasn't wrong. Three weeks later Guy received an Aria Award for his single 'Angels Brought Me Here', which was the biggest selling song of 2004.

Some people I talk to are cynical about the Australian Idol TV series; however, I have a different viewpoint. The massive exposure of television gives a once-in-a-lifetime chance to new young talent to achieve their dreams. It promotes a great industry and creates local heroes. There is nothing wrong with this. Aussies needs to get behind their own and bury the tall-poppy syndrome for good! Some of the world's best talents, whether it's actors, sportspeople, musicians, authors or business entrepreneurs, are Australians. Come on Aussie – come on!

Zero to hero

It's interesting to observe what it takes to go from zero to hero. Nothing demonstrates this phenomenon more clearly than the music industry. The way in which the creation of music from the 'dream makers' connects with a global audience of 'dream takers', can be a fascinating journey of failure and success. The old adage – *Success is a journey not a destination* – is so true in this case.

My years in the music industry have led me to understand that major success in artistry and communication doesn't happen overnight. If you observe the careers of most superstar recording artists you will see that it takes two to three albums before an artist records a body of work that produces a career-defining moment. It can take years of performing and recording to develop a work that takes a performer from zero to hero. This is a fundamental fact of life. It takes time, talent and experience mixed with opportunity and persistence to achieve ultimate success.

Boz is the buzz

One of my all time favourite albums is Boz Scaggs's soul-pop fused *Silk Degrees*. I worked with Boz during my CBS years, as Australia gave him his early success. Boz recorded his first album in the mid-sixties but made little impact. He then played for several years with The Steve Miller Band. In 1976, he collaborated with two LA session musicians, David Paich, and Jeff Porcaro (who later went on to form Toto, with notable success). *Silk Degrees* became a worldwide classic recording, a killer album that contained three hit singles and was an early career highlight for me – a real buzz.

Silk Degrees remained on the Australian charts for 102 weeks.

Killer to thriller

Michael Jackson's *Thriller* became the world's biggest selling record, yet it was Jackson's second solo album. He had previously recorded over a dozen albums with his brothers, The Jackson Five.

Thriller has sold over 56 000 000 units globally (in all formats) since its 1983 release and was number one on the US Billboard album charts for an unprecedented thirty-seven weeks.

The piano man

When I first met Billy Joel he was a talented singer-songwriter who had just recorded 'The Piano Man', but it was his fourth album, *The Stranger*, which contained the career-defining ballad 'Just the Way You Are' that took his music to the world.

A hot August night

Neil Diamond began his career as a budding composer in New York's Tin Pan Alley writing songs for other people. 'I'm a Believer' for The Monkeys was an early success. Years later he wrote and recorded *Hot August Night,* which became one of the most admired live recordings in music history.

In 1976 one in four Australian households owned a copy of *Hot August Night.*

Saturday night fever

The Bee Gees' career was in a spiral until that defining period when they recorded a bunch of hit songs that became the soundtrack for *Saturday Night Fever,* an album that epitomised the disco era of the seventies. The record went on to become the biggest selling soundtrack album of all time and gave the Brothers Gibb a place in the history books of rock 'n' roll.

Over a four-decade period The Bee Gees would sell over 100 000 000 recordings.

Each of these performers began with *good* songs and, by continually performing and recording, produced *better* material until they developed their *best* recorded work. Each process was connected to the next. While all of these examples demonstrate the music that affected *my* life, there is a sense of history being created with each step in these artists' magnificent careers.

And sometimes history has an uncanny way of repeating itself.

The war of the worlds

In 1898, HG Wells wrote *The War of the Worlds.* It became a literary classic.

In 1938 a brilliant young broadcaster called Orson Welles, (no relation) threw much of the eastern seaboard of America into panic with his vividly realistic radio adaptation of H G Wells's book about an alien invasion. At a time when Europe was about to be plunged into World War II, such was the realism of his documentary, that many Americans were convinced that an invasion was actually taking place. Although Orson Welles became an acclaimed actor/director, this dramatised event made him famous.

Over sixty years later Steven Spielberg, Hollywood's master storyteller, transformed Wells's epic tale into a blockbuster movie with Tom Cruise doing battle with the Martian fighting machines.

I have a personal connection with this story as I played a central role in introducing Jeff Wayne's musical adaptation of *The War of the Worlds* to Australia.

It was back in 1978. I was director of marketing for CBS Records Australia and was in Los Angeles attending one of those 'infamous' CBS Records conventions. Over dinner a mature English gent introduced himself as Jerry Wayne. I was soon to discover he was Jeff Wayne's father. Jeff had enjoyed a successful UK recording career as David Essex's producer, and had just composed, orchestrated, arranged, conducted and produced a musical interpretation of the H G Wells masterpiece.

Through this chance meeting with Mr Wayne senior I contacted Jeff and invited him to come to Australia to promote his new work. The album had just been released in Oz and we all believed at CBS that it had the potential to be a big hit. However we needed to find a way to create significant media attention. Concept albums were difficult to promote because they were not radio friendly. One month later Jeff Wayne arrived 'down under.' I won't go into detail here, because I told the tale about this piece of marketing history in my first book. The album however, went to number one in Australia, and achieved multi platinum status, selling 800 000 double albums over the next two decades. *The War of the Worlds* sold 13 000 000 units globally.

Fast forward to July 2005

The blockbuster movie is opening in cinemas around Australia and (unbeknown to me,) Jeff Wayne is back in the country to promote a new digitally remastered collectors' edition of his musical masterpiece, to a new generation of listeners. Out of the blue, I received a call from my CBS pals (now Sony/BMG) informing me that an old 'Martian mate' wanted to say gidday! Amazingly, twenty seven years had passed since Jeff and I had last met. What was more amazing was that he remembered! The reconnection was 'out of this world'!

With a sense of déjà vú, Jeff accepted my invitation to do a live phone interview with me on my 4BC radio segment the following evening. He recounted the story of how he convinced actor Richard Burton to read the narration, and how he assembled the disparate talents of David Essex, Julie Covington, Justin Haywood (Moody Blues), Phil Lynott (Thin Lizzy) and Chris Thompson (Manfred Mann) to perform on the record.

After all these years it was a fascinating piece of archival music history. And compelling live radio! The next day our shop buzzed with sales of the new 'War' – it was all happening again! A few days later a personally autographed copy of Jeff's new product arrived for me and as I opened this stunning collector's edition, the following inscription read ...Barry... Here we go again! ... Jeff .

What you give out always comes back in some way and at some time.

Connecting the content

The definitive work of these artists all had great content. And content is king. Each song was a performance that was a prelude to the next. The best example of this is The Beatles' *Sergeant Pepper's* and The Beach Boys' *Pet Sounds* albums. Both these recordings were sixties masterpieces. They weren't just a collection of songs. Each album was a complete musical thought.

These albums were released within six months of each other and set new standards in modern music. They raised the creative bar to previously unheard of levels – some would argue they haven't been matched since.

It seems to me that success is greatest when all the elements are correctly connected as one. I view business in much the same way. It's the successful development of procedures that work together with the correct placement of the right people in the right place and at the right time so that the content (goods and services) are easily connected to the market.

The challenge in writing this book was not just developing the content, but importantly connecting all my *Bullisms* together. They then equalled the sum of the parts of my *Bullseye Principle,* which, as we know, asks you to:

1. **Set your sights**

2. **Plan the process**

3. **Implement the strategy**

4. **Deal with the issues**

5. **Measure performance**

6. **Be disciplined and determined**

7. **Hit the Bullseye**

Each process is *connected* to the others.

Connecting the dots

I am blessed to have five wonderful grandchildren and one of the pleasurable roles of grandparenting is to share experiences with inquisitive young minds. Often I find the roles reverse, because the innocence of youth can be a great teacher.

I was recently assisting our young four-year-old grandson to play the game of connecting the dots. The idea was to use a crayon to connect dots to form a familiar image. This is an effective way to teach a young mind to recognise that each piece of information is somehow connected to form a total picture. My grandson's reward was to colour in the final familiar image with his crayons to complete the big picture. At the same time his older brother was working at a jigsaw puzzle which contained the same learning sequence. His eventual shout of excitement was a result of many hours of putting the right pieces in the right places.

It occurred to me that business is much the same. It's understanding that each circumstance or experience is somehow connected, each process is *connected* to the other. It's a matter of connecting the dots.

If we correctly connect all the elements of business fundamentals together in the right way, then they will all fall into place. It's realising that a connection exists, in business and in life. Some people never find it, while others seamlessly connect one piece to another. It's these connections that allow people to get what they want, by helping others get what *they* want. Winners get what they want by helping others. Good team leaders know this because it is the first fundamental of developing a winning team: connecting the right people in the right jobs so that their performance supports others, allows you to achieve the team objectives.

Understanding that each problem, adversity, opportunity, or challenge, is linked to every other problem, opportunity, etc., in some way assists with the development of suitable solutions and strategies.

Here are some of my strategies that deal with the daily issues; the problems, the opportunities, the challenges and solutions. These are my crayons that connect the dots to create the big picture.

- Solve problems – achieve your goals.
- Create don't compete – innovate don't imitate.
- Change is not a threat, but an opportunity.
- Persistence always defeats resistance.
- You don't have to be the biggest to be the best.
- No is Negotiable.

Sound familiar? Of course they do. They are my *Bullisms!* And hopefully they make this text fun, easy to read, and memor-a-Bull. That's my strategy. My *Bullisms* are not only my business philosophies; they are marketing tools for a brand for which I can claim ownership, a brand that differentiates this 'Little Bull' … from all the udders!

BULLET POINTS

- You never know what is waiting around the next bend.
- Intuition is a powerful instinct. If only we'd take notice of it more often.
- Things work out best for people who make the best of the way things work out.
- Things aren't always as good as they look – or as bad as they seem.
- Success is a journey not a destination.
- Winners get what they want by helping others get what they want.

Chapter 11

Effective marketing

BULLISM:™ MARKET-A-BULL

Market makers are market takers.

Retail chestnut

The dictionary defines marketing as: 'the business activity of presenting products or services to potential customers in such a way as to make them eager to buy.'

My personal marketing philosophy is simply this:

Effective marketing is the successful connection of advertising, promotion, publicity, merchandising and product, in the right way at the right time.

Let me explain my interpretation of each of these valuable components, and how they all connect to create effective marketing.

Advertising

Advertising targets the media best suited to getting your brand and your message across to your customer demographic. It is costly but is the most effective way to brand your business and drive sales. Advertising should be a budgeted expense. I always negotiate advertising support with suppliers of the products that I plan to promote. Whether its print, broadcast or internet, the media is an essential part of the marketing effort.

Promotion

Promotion is the development of ideas, strategies and campaigns which will draw attention to your brand and product, involving your customer uniquely with your goods and services offer. Our artist celebrity appearances are an example of a high-profile promotional experience.

Publicity

Publicity is the unpaid media exposure of yourself and your business to build awareness about your goods and services and to profile your brand. It's important to know the difference between advertising and publicity. Advertising is within your control because you are paying for the service. Publicity is about managing your image and building community awareness of your business activities, which massages the marketing message.

Merchandising

Merchandising is the placement of product in the right place at the right time. It should be well signed, well lit, creatively displayed and coincide with the marketing campaign.

Every business places different values on its marketing; however, we have always achieved our best marketing results by the coordination of *all* of the above components with the product offer.

Product

Effective marketing is developing a process that makes a good idea or product or service easily accessible to the market. I often advise young musicians that writing good material is one thing, getting people to listen to it is another. Good content without good exposure is simply not good enough.

Author Robert Kiyosaki demonstrated this big-time. The content of his best-selling book *Rich Dad, Poor Dad* was good, but so was the marketing. Two dads with conflicting attitudes towards money was a simple but effective way to expose different philosophies about wealth creation.

The *Australian Idol* competition was more than a talent quest because it had the power of television to turn unknown young talent into household names.

Sir Richard Branson continually flaunts his Virgin brand in varied industries with clever marketing of a well-known global identity. Steve Irwin transformed an unknown zoo into an international tourist attraction by marketing himself as *The Crocodile Hunter*.

They all started as a good idea that became a product or service that people wanted.

In all the cases we've been discussing, they all used exceptional marketing to gain huge public appeal, and the brand builders became household names. Once good exposure is achieved, the next critical step is good distribution. Clever marketers know that once a product successfully breaks onto the market, the key is to maximise sales and drive the product through the roof.

Make the big ones bigger

When I was marketing director at CBS Records back in the late seventies, our objective was to create big-selling records. The big sellers always compensated for the flops and funded the development of new artists. Our marketing battle cry was 'make the big ones *bigger*!'

One of the mechanisms of the record business is to select a single off an album, get airplay for the song and make it a hit. Hopefully the album becomes a big seller. Singles have always been the most important promotion tool for the successful marketing of albums. Over the years, while music styles have changed, this promotion fundamental has not. Singles sell albums. While our competitors were satisfied with one hit single off an album we would develop a strategy to make several songs off the same record big hits. Therefore the album would continue to be in the charts for up to a year sometimes. This would drive the product into multi-platinum sales. Boz Scaggs's *Silk Degrees*, Meatloaf's *Bat Out Of Hell*, Jeff Wayne's *War of the Worlds*, Neil Diamond's *Beautiful Noise*, ELO's *Discovery* and Michael Jackson's *Off the Wall*, were all mega-sellers during my years at CBS.

Here is a more recent example of how well the music business understands that creative marketing is the successful connection of advertising, promotion, publicity, merchandising and product, in the right place at the right time.

Popular Canadian crooner Michael Bublé and Il Divo (four classically trained superstar tenors) released new product in March 2005. With support from their respective record labels, six weeks later both acts were in Australia for a short but hectic promotion tour. They performed exclusive (but separate) showcases to media and retail, and tirelessly did the rounds of press and radio promotion that culminated in both acts performing live on the national Logies telecast. On the same program TV advertising was placed to promote their new albums, simultaneous to merchandising and stock placement at retail. One week later was Mothers day, one of the most important gift giving times of the year for music. The timing was perfect and because all the elements of the marketing plan worked collectively the impact was huge. Michael Bublé and Il Divo became the perfect gifts for Mum.

However, it didn't stop there. This was only the beginning of a long marketing campaign to make big sellers – BIGGER! During the next six months both acts were back in the country for live national tours and the same marketing formula applied again. This time, however, with the intention of building both these albums into big Christmas sellers. This marketing muscle not only builds artist careers, it also cultivates market awareness for their next product cycle. This is what I mean by effective marketing.

Over the years Denis Handlin, Sony Chairman and CEO, has fuelled his company using this strategy of making the big ones bigger. Look what Sony Music has done with Michael Jackson, Mariah Carey, Celine Dion, Pearl Jam and in recent years Pete Murray and Delta Goodrum. All mega-sellers. Denis also never gives up on a piece of music once it becomes a hit. That's why Sony is a great record company and Denis Handlin is one of the country's best music industry executives.

Denis and I began our careers together back in 1970 at The Australian Record Company. Within a few years ARC became CBS Records and eventually Sony Music. Recently, I had dinner with Denis to celebrate his appointment as CEO of Sony/BMG Entertainment Australia, and to enjoy our long friendship. We discussed the qualities and talent needed for a new generation of emerging hit makers.

So you wanna be a star?

Record companies have always searched for stars. The process will continue because of the public's thirst for celebrities. TV programs like *Australian Idol* have made the process of 'star-making' public. This is not a bad thing because it is the public in the end who decides whether they like the artist, will attend their concerts and buy their product. To build short-term success into a long-term career, however, requires a basic understanding of what creates success in the music business.

It's about being a *role model*; being someone that others want to be like. Kylie and Delta have inspired a generation of 'I wanna be like you' fans and they understand the influence their stardom has on others.

It's about writing good songs – *content is king.* If you can write your own material then publishing control is a valuable asset to the artist and the record company. Write songs people want to hear and especially write for radio. Self-indulgent musicians who record music for themselves can alienate the mainstream. If you can't get airplay in this country then it may not happen. And *Australian Idol* and *Neighbours* won't last forever!

Surround yourself with *competent management* who understand how to get a record deal and how to stage-manage your development – importantly someone who knows the difference between the music business and the business of music!

The Bullseye Principle is a good template for building a successful career in the *music* business because its structure deals with the *business* of music.

Finally have a *work ethic* and be prepared to do what it takes to achieve your dream. Keep your feet on the ground, leave egos at the door of opportunity, be prepared to learn from others and work hard.

I have often said that my mentors are not the Donald Trumps of the world.

If this was the case I would have been *fired* long ago! They are the artists who have built long careers by nurturing talent and mostly working hard at it for as long as it takes. Such an artist is Michael Crawford.

Michael's durable career spans four decades with multiple movie, TV and Broadway roles to his credit including *Hello Dolly* with Barbra Streisand, as the incorrigible Frank Spencer in the long-running TV comedy series *Some Mothers Do 'Ave 'Em*, and his highly acclaimed performance as the phantom in *The Phantom of the Opera*. However, it wasn't until the early nineties that the world discovered that Frank Spencer had a great voice.

I first met Michael in 1993 when he came to Toombul to promote a new album. He had just wrapped up the highly successful season of *The Phantom of the Opera* in New York and was in Australia on a concert tour. He returned again in 2001. I then had the opportunity to interview him on stage in front of a thousand fans.

As I introduced Michael I became aware of the absolute professionalism of the man and how he skilfully used his charisma and loveable personality. I told the story of this famous interview in *A Little Bull*; however, *this* story is about the man's work ethic and dedication to perfection, how he relentlessly rehearses and never gives up until he gets it right.

After an exhausting two hours of product signing I had a short chat with Michael over a coffee in Westfield's private boardroom. It was fascinating and, not to miss a minute, I even chatted with him as I showed him to the bathroom. He must have thought I was a real Wally!

In everyone's life there is a defining moment when somebody says something that has a profound impact. For me that moment had arrived. That person was Michael Crawford.

What he said gave me the strength to proceed with my career ambition to become a professional business speaker. I must confess, for a long time I had serious self-doubt that I was good enough. I am a retailer after all, not necessarily an entertainer – there's a big difference! But if necessity is the mother of invention, then I was about to reinvent myself!

Michael explained that his life had been one of challenges and he had to work at every opportunity that was offered to him. He said that when a part in a movie or a Broadway show presented itself, the only way to be the best at the part was to rehearse until he *became* the part. It sounded awfully like the *good, better, best* of my *Bullseye Principle*.

In his internationally acclaimed 1999 best-selling autobiography, *Parcel Arrived Safely; Tied With String*, Michael wrote how he got the part of the phantom. He explained that in 1984, he casually bumped into composer Andrew Lloyd Webber at interval during one of Andrew's new Broadway shows. In casual conversation Andrew mentioned the possibility of Michael doing a role in his new work in progress *The Phantom of the Opera*. Michael told him that he would be very interested. After that night, however, he never heard another word about it. He later heard that half the world was auditioning for the part.

In 1986 Michael's agent received a call asking if he was still interested in the role of the phantom. It was Sarah Brightman (who became the female lead in *The Phantom*) who'd heard Michael taking singing lessons. She recommended him to Andrew Lloyd Webber. Michael worked for weeks rehearsing for the role he desperately wanted and when the audition day came, it was obvious to the famous composer that he had found his phantom. Michael explained: 'Deep down I could do it. Thus began a new regime of singing lessons, practising five and six hours a day, and two-hour sessions with my teacher every single day of the week for the next two months.' And it paid off. Michael Crawford became known the world over as *The Phantom*. This ignited a significant recording career.

Michael and I finished our coffee and as I walked with him to his car I thanked him for a great day. His appearance had been a huge success. He grinned at me and said that this was the first time he'd been interviewed by a retailer and he was a bit apprehensive at first. I said: 'Mate – not as apprehensive as me. I was terrified!' We both laughed. It was then that I asked him the question that was to have a big impact on my future.

I said, 'Michael, you handled the interview so well and today has been such a success. Please tell me what it takes to be as professional as you?' He said:

'Barry, just hard work. If you want something badly enough, then work at it, practise and rehearse it until it is *you* people want to hear.' What he told me was that he was like everyone else; he had to work at his talent because nothing comes easy.

He told me that he was being interviewed by Ray Martin on Channel Nine the following evening. He said he knew what he would be saying to Ray tomorrow. 'You've prepared for it?' I said. Michael gave me a knowing wink as we said goodbye.

The next night I was one of the million viewers who watched *An Evening With Michael Crawford*, and was enthralled by his comic, charismatic and flawless performance. He even gave a very funny display of having a prostate examination which put Ray Martin out of control! After performing three songs from his new album, the program became a ratings winner for the network.

I knew then the meaning of what Michael had told me. If you are going to be exposed to an audience then work at the performer in you, and give the performance of your life – every time. And it takes preparation.

A few days before Michael's appearance at Toombul, he visited the centre and checked out the store and the stage where we were presenting him. I now knew the reason for this. He was rehearsing the performance and leaving nothing to chance. What a pro.

And so I completely reworked my speaking presentation. Using Powerpoint technology I introduced my business *Hit List* into my presentation, wrote a book around it to gain exposure and profile and studied the craft of public speaking from seasoned veterans. And I just worked and worked at it. I am still working at it!

I arrive early at the venue where I am to speak, do the necessary preparation such as sound, video, lighting rehearsals, and familiarise myself with the room and the audience as they arrive. When I take the stage I have the mindset that 'this is going to be the best presentation that this audience has ever heard'.

This is what I learned that day from Michael Crawford. But this lesson also applies to anyone wanting to win a client and close a sale. Arrive early for the appointment, be well prepared for the presentation and give the performance of your life!

The art of the ad

So far my *Bullisms* have covered customer service, sales, branding, promotion, and publicity, so let's look at the next (and most costly) ingredient that makes up the marketing mix – advertising.

Leo Burnett, founder of Leo Burnett Advertising, once wrote: 'The sole purpose of business is service. The sole purpose of advertising is explaining the service which business renders.'

What are we selling?

Have you ever asked yourself during the TV ad breaks ... 'What was that all about? What are they selling?' If I have to sit through some of the mindless tirades of television commercials, I'd at least like to know what it is they are promoting. Some of them I just don't get. I suspect that they are created by some advertising guru imagining he or she is a Hollywood director making a thirty-second TV movie and hell bent on winning the next award for creative brilliance! OK, maybe that's a bit cynical, but do they always work, do they sell product, or do they simply waste the client's money?

Some work by repetition, others by clever scriptwriting and others by that four letter word– *sale*. Many, I suspect, fail to pay for their expensive production and media budgets; costs will continue to increase, but will viewer numbers increase? Unlikely, I also suspect, because of market fragmentation. The time is fast approaching, with the introduction of high definition digital subscription television (providing viewers with unlimited choice and content), that consumer support for commercial TV will be challenged and audience availability for advertising will fragment. Advertisers will have a more difficult task of getting the bang for their ad bucks. Anyway, back to the main game. What are we selling?

It was once written that advertising is nothing more than salesmanship

The plumber was flooded with calls!

multiplied by a mass medium. It is a good salesperson who is able to close hundreds of sales at one time, again and again. Doesn't it make sense then to get the best sales advice from master salespeople and then apply their tactics to a mass marketing medium? I certainly find it difficult to discover master salespeople in ad agencies these days. This is why we control our own advertising and buy media direct.

I am not suggesting you do this because we can't be good at everything, and outsourcing advertising to the experts allows time to do what you do best and that is to manage your business. Advertising in my view, however, is not an expense, it is an investment. Managing my business means controlling my business investment, and marketing costs are an investment that require management. I never allow my advertising costs (which I share with my suppliers) to get tangled up in my fixed expenses (wages and rent) in my balance sheet. I view advertising like stock. I invest money to make money. Because it's my money I don't trust it to people who don't share the same values. This is why I remain cautious about many ad agencies. Never lose sight of the number-one rule of advertising – give customers a reason to choose you.

It's not what you say it's how you say it!

Ken O'Flaherty operates the *Buderim Chronicle*, a small community newspaper on Queensland's Sunshine Coast. Understandably, advertising is the *Chronicle's* main revenue source and Ken likes to see his ads work for his customers. One of his clients is a local plumbing contractor who placed an advertisement that promoted his services. The ad copy contained too much information. Ken told his client it needed to be kept simple. His client disagreed because he had written the copy. Predictably it didn't work and the plumber withdrew his advertising. Ken suggested that he would rewrite the copy for the plumber and run the ad again. If it didn't work this time then he wouldn't pay for it. Ken simplified the copy to ten words:

Dripping tap? Leaking toilet? Smelly bathroom?

We can help you.

The plumber was flooded with calls!

Whenever I contemplate spending my hard-earned dollars on advertising I continually question the cost versus the result, and it gets tougher as competition grows. Why advertise the same as everyone else with the only distinction being price? But why promote at all unless we know who our customer is and what it is they want? Smart marketers identify their market and then tell it the *benefits* of how their product will improve their customers' lifestyle and satisfy their needs. This creates the desire to embrace the proposition. Advertising is the way to communicate these benefits. For example:

Product	Benefit
Plasma television	Sell the experience of owning a home theatre.
Musical instrument	Sell the joy of playing in a band.
Sporting equipment	Sell the fun of playing in a team.
Computer	Sell the business solution.
Tickets to the footy	Sell the idea of a great family day with the kids.

By selling the added value and lifestyle benefits that your product provides means that price is not the only consideration.

Take a look at the great brands of the world and you will find that by clever marketing they stand for more than the product itself. Harley Davidson is the pride of ownership; Nike is a fashion statement and it's cool to wear the 'swoosh'; Disney is a family tradition; RM Williams is an Aussie outback experience and The Flight Centre targets holidays, not flying. Each brand targets a customer they know and sets their sights on market domination. Some brands become tourist attractions, such as Guinness, which is Ireland's national treasure. The same goes for whisky in Scotland. And who *hasn't* been to Disneyland!

So when I consider advertising, it is with three objectives in mind.

1. First and foremost it is to sell product.

2. Second is to build the brand.

3. Third is to differentiate from the competition.

I then make an advertisement that delivers on those objectives, always underpinning the customer's 'need to know' rules. The four 'Ws':

1. What they want.

2. When they want it.

3. Where they want it.

4. Why they want it.

Effective marketers are those who are close to the product and close to the customer. Once they know the answer to the four 'Ws' then the delivery promise becomes:

1. What they will pay for it.

2. When they can have it.

3. Where they can get it.

4. Why they need it.

Whatever you are marketing, always ask: 'What is it you are really selling?' and 'Who is your customer?' This is not rocket science. Consumers are time poor, confused by all the mixed messages and need to be led. If you don't tell them who you are, what you are doing, why they need your product and how they can get it, they will ignore you and go to someone who will. Market takers are those who understand how to deepen their relationship with their customers.

High-performing businesses all have clear brand strategies and their marketing is fuelled by a deep understanding of their customers, which is supported by superior service.

Read the last sentence again, because it contains three powerful messages that simplify effective marketing.

BULLET POINTS

- Good content without good exposure is simply not good enough.

- If you want something badly enough then work at it, practise and rehearse it until it is *you* people want to hear.

- Work at the performer in you, and give the performance of your life – every time.

- The sole purpose of business is service. The sole purpose of advertising is explaining the service that business renders.

- It's not what you say it's how you say it.

- Effective marketers are those who are close to the product and even closer to the customer.

THE BULLSEYE PRINCIPLE™

4 DEAL WITH THE ISSUES

SOLVE PROBLEMS, SEIZE OPPORTUNITIES

Chapter 12

Customer service is everything

BULLISM: SERVICE-A-BULL

It is the service we are not obliged to give that people value the most.

James C. Penney

I believe there are only two kinds of businesses: those that understand how to connect to their customers and those that don't. Customer service is everything and no matter what business we are in, service is paramount. Good businesses sell to their customers. Great businesses connect with them.

Effective customer connection means repeat business and we all know that the customer who keeps coming back is the most profitable. Yet so many businesses fail to understand that emotion is the key component of the connection process. What is the key emotional experience? It's the service experience! It's not just a matter of 'best price'; often it's a case of 'best service'.

Best price customers are not always profitable customers and we let our competition argue over them. People who embrace 'best service' are *our* customers because they place a value on service and are prepared to pay a little more to get it.

Why is that, you ask? Well, good service is hard to find nowadays and that is why the customer always remembers the service long after the price. The mass market notion of promoting 'lower prices every day' has pushed good old customer service into the waste bin. Best prices with best service are a rare commodity. They just don't go together in today's 'stack 'em high and watch 'em fly' merchant mentality. So here lies the fundamental distinction between product and service businesses. You just need to decide which team you're on.

Big business thrives on the 'sell *more* for less' model.

Our specialty business is based on the 'sell *less* for more' model.

Nowadays my schedule does not permit me to work in our business every day, or should I say more accurately that I choose not to, because it is capably managed by my family. I am, however, easily accessible by mobile phone. While writing this Bullism on customer service in my home office, I was deliberating over how I could explain the critical importance of how service supports repeat business, and more importantly, how I could emphasise it from a practitioner's daily experience. After all I am not a theorist, I work in real time.

While I was thinking, I received a call on my mobile from a widow in Clayfield, an affluent Brisbane suburb not far from our store. I don't believe in coincidence. Things happen for a reason. Obviously this example of customer service was meant to be included. She phoned to thank me for the service that one of our people had extended to her and was very emotional in her appreciation of our service ethic. Apparently her VCR was malfunctioning and needed reprogramming. We are well aware how technology baffles some senior citizens. Our young salesperson called by on his way home and solved the problem.

I always encourage our team to do that 'little extra'. It's part of our training ethic. As a result, I receive numerous goodwill calls from satisfied clients.

The lady from Clayfield had been considering updating to a DVD player and purchased one from us the very next day. Now don't miss the point here because obviously our service support prompted a new sale. However, she told others about our diligent young salesman and before long most of her neighbours also ended up with new technology from us.

Word of mouth is the best advertising because it costs nothing and it leads to referrals. And referral business is good business. Interestingly, most of our up-market home cinema business is won by referral. Repeat or referral customers are the most profitable because there are no acquisition costs. It's what you do after you do what you're expected to do that matters most.

The loan phone

Here is an example of doing that little bit more than people expect. I was preparing to leave for Melbourne to speak at a conference for one of Australia's biggest corporations. In my haste I dropped my mobile phone and not surprisingly it wouldn't work. I needed my phone that day and pondered what to do because I had less than two hours before my flight departed. I called my Telstra account representative, Jacqui, and told her my dilemma, hoping she could help me out. She said that she would try to get me a loan phone, but doubted if she could get it to me before I departed. Just as I was about to leave the shop for the airport a courier arrived with the loan phone from Jacqui. I was delighted and I knew how I could reward her.

Whenever I am engaged to speak at a conference I endeavour to relate to my audience by way of a personal experience. I also try to find a connection mechanism that allows me to speak *with* my audience not *to* them on a subject that is familiar to them. There is a big difference. Good presenters communicate their message in an entertaining yet motivating way and once an audience relationship is established the message is well received and retained.

What Jacqui didn't know (because I didn't tell her), was *that* day I was engaged to speak at a Telstra national sales conference! And what I *didn't* know was her immediate superiors were at the conference!

To add a theatrical touch I placed the loan phone on the lectern for all to see. When I came to the part of my presentation on customer service, I told the delegates about an impressive customer service experience I had had that morning. The audience came alive as I held the loan phone high in the air

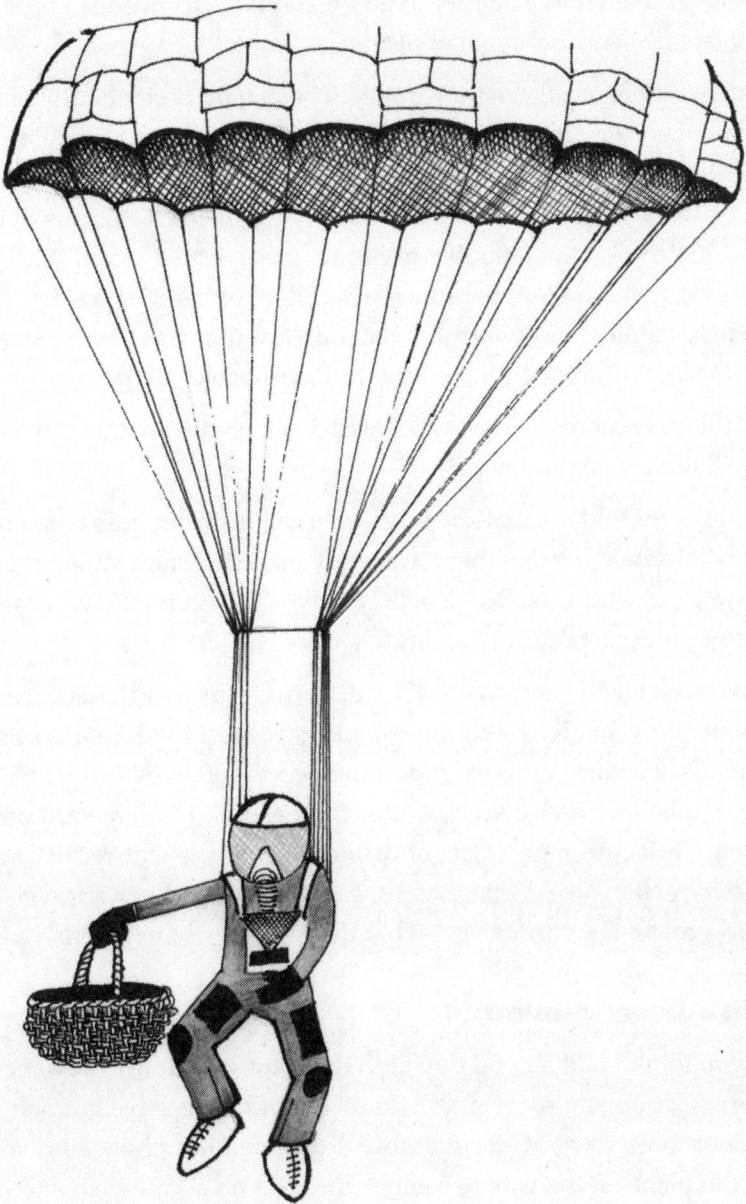

I had received great service from one of their corporate dealerships.

and told them how I had received great service from one of *their* corporate dealerships and from one of *their* salespeople.

At the time, I recall Telstra was being beaten up pretty badly by the media about their service standards in 'the bush'. It came as a refreshing change to the delegation to hear someone actually singing Telstra's praises. The table of Brisbane execs went berserk when they realised it was one of their team and snatched at their mobiles to call an unsuspecting Jacqui. My timing was so good that this story became the highlight of the Telstra sales conference. In fact, I almost lost control of an audience that was having so much fun; it was like running with the bulls at Pamplona!

At this very moment, however, I was dealing with another situation which I will tell you about later.

Jacqui later told me that she received a call from her boss who enthusiastically informed her that there was a guy up on the stage telling the delegates how great she was! Not surprisingly, she received five more calls of congratulations during the day.

One week later Jacqui received a call from Optus (who had heard the story) to offer her a job. Telstra countered and gave Jacqui a promotion. She became one of their most successful account representatives that year. Wow, did I get unbelieve-a-bull service after that! All I did was reward an excellent example of customer service and, like most people who receive a satisfying service experience, I told everyone about it. Good news travels fast. As I said previously, winners get what they want by helping others.

My lips are sealed

If you think I had a good day at that Telstra conference, however, you are wrong. There are some days when I should have stayed in bed. This was one of those days. It started when I dropped my phone and smashed it. In the plane on the way to Melbourne, I bit on a sandwich and one of my front crowns broke off a tooth and fell onto my lap. Murphy's Law was active that day!

When I arrived at Melbourne airport I immediately called my dentist (thanks to Jacqui's loan phone) and told him my dilemma. I informed him that I had to present at a conference within the hour and had lost a front tooth! As there was no time to find a local dentist he suggested that I stick the cap back in with super glue. I said, 'Are you serious? Will it work?'

He said 'There are no guarantees!' I didn't like the sound of it.

I raced off to the airport newsagent, bought a tube of superglue and then bolted for the nearest men's room to do the repair. I have since found out that you should never put super glue near your mouth. Particularly if you've got a big mouth like mine. As I had my mouth open looking in the mirror, glue in one hand, tooth in the other, this guy came in, assessed the situation and started to laugh. I must have looked a real dill! Being distracted I accidentally dropped some glue onto my lips. As soon as I closed my mouth my lips stuck together and I couldn't open them! Imagine this. A professional presenter on the way to speak at a big conference and I couldn't open my bloody mouth! Have you ever heard anything so ridiculous? A public speaker with his lips sealed!

By the time I managed to open my mouth some skin came off my bottom lip and my tongue decided to get into the act. It got stuck also! Bugger ... I was in a mess! I must have looked ridiculous! After what seemed a painful few minutes I managed to glue the tooth back in and clean myself up. Later during the Telstra presentation when I held the phone up high to deliver the punch line, guess what happened? You got it! The crown fell out, and during the excitement of the moment I nearly swallowed it!

Fortunately the audience was so excited about their heroine (Jacqui) that they hardly noticed me quickly pocketing the sticky culprit. Predictably, I didn't smile the rest of the conference. There are days when I should stay in bed.

Some days are diamonds

While some days are difficult others are diamonds. Over the years, our business reputation grew as we ramped up the presentation of celebrities and entertainers. One such famous entertainer was John Denver.

It was back in 1988 and John Denver was on an Australian concert tour. He had agreed to do an album signing with us promoting his latest musical offering, *Some Days Are Diamonds*. When John arrived at the shopping centre he appeared apprehensive and he told me that he didn't like doing shopping centre appearances. I assumed he had a previous bad experience as he was clearly uncomfortable and a little moody.

However, this is not an unusual reaction from a superstar whose main domain is the stage of a concert hall, not a suburban shopping centre. I had many issues to deal with early on, in order to gain the credibility needed for superstar entertainers to agree to do product signings and performances with us. Once we overcame the problems of security, presentation, production and marketing, however, a successful format fell into place.

As I spoke reassuringly to him prior to his appearance, I asked John about the defining moment in his remarkable career. I enjoy asking this question because it usually provokes a fascinating answer. I have discovered that the majority of the superstar entertainers that I have worked with are really nice people, who began their career in a most humble way.

He replied that it was his composition 'Leaving on a Jet Plane' (which became an international chart topper for Peter, Paul and Mary in the sixties) that got him noticed. It was the 1971 album *Poems Prayers and Promises*, however, that established him as a solo performer. His biography highlights how he achieved superstardom, thanks to the million-selling hits 'Take Me Home Country Roads' and 'Sunshine on My Shoulders'.

His 1974 *Best of* collection sold over 10 000 000 copies worldwide and remained on the charts for over two years.

It was an emotional day for John Denver fans, and as he relaxed into the CD signing, he appeared to enjoy the occasion. Several thousand people turned up to welcome him and nothing pleases an entertainer more than a full house. It was John Denver's personal appearance, however, that established for me a successful format in presenting superstars on the centre stage of Toombul Shoppingtown. Cliff Richard had made his debut appearance just six months earlier and the organisation and promotion for these two events was massive. We gained a reputation with Westfield, record companies and

Customer service is everything

tour promoters that personal appearances could attract huge crowds, would sell heaps of product and promote the artists' concerts. They were secure and successful events and everyone benefited. This set the scene for many more musical milestones in our retail journey at Toombul.

That evening I attended John's stunning concert. His unique songs and clear vocals captivated an audience eager for a night of memorable entertainment. Afterwards, backstage, John gave me the nod of approval for a well-organised event. He then told me the reason for his apprehension was because he had never done a shopping centre appearance before!

I recall that the 'guitar man' and my good mate, Tommy Emmanuel, was the opening act of that John Denver concert. Tommy and I reminisced about the occasion recently when he called in to do a performance for us and spotted a photo of John and me on our 'Toombul Wall of Fame'.

I related to Tommy the powerful emotional experience John gave to all the fans who came to Toombul on that memorable day. Tommy told me it was a personal career highlight for him to work with such a brilliant singer-songwriter.

Sadly tragedy struck John Denver on 12 October 1997 when his experimental aircraft suddenly crashed, killing him instantly at the age of fifty-three. John became one of the most beloved entertainers of his era and is missed by fans world wide. He remains with us through his musical legacy.

Leaving on a jet plane

As you can tell I have two obvious passions in my business life. One is the passion for the *music* and the other is for my *business*. This combination is the *music business* I love, and is why I have been a participant most of my life. To stay true to my passion it is important to express myself in these same balanced terms in this book. I hope you find my celebrity stories interesting because each of these entertainers wove their musical magic into my life and their stories all contain relevant business messages to be interpreted in their own special way.

John Denver's first composition, 'Leaving on a Jet Plane', reminds me of an interesting story with such a message.

It was the autumn of 2003, and I was 'leaving on a jet plane' bound for New Zealand and was involved in an emotional customer-service experience in a most unusual way. I was travelling from Brisbane to Christchurch, where I was speaking at a business convention the next day. After waiting a considerable time at the Qantas departure lounge for my outgoing flight, an announcement was made that the flight was to be delayed and a new departure time was unscheduled.

The lounge was full of departing passengers who began to react to the disappointing news. The loudest reaction predictably came from a group of Americans obviously returning to the US of A. They wore huge stetsons and their Texan drawls were almost as wide as their belt buckles, which resembled the hubcaps on a good V8.

After a second announcement indicating that the flight would be two hours late, the mood in the lounge darkened. Qantas had a problem. What they did, however, was to turn an ugly situation into a customer-service exercise … à la carte. They did not offer free drinks to pacify the contrary patrons. Instead a senior Qantas official, dressed in an immaculate flight uniform, came into the lounge and asked for the passengers' attention. He looked impressive, but what he did next was more impressive.

He was holding an aluminium canister, which was obviously a mechanical device of some kind. He introduced himself as the captain of our aircraft and after apologising for the late departure, he explained the reason for the delay. With a commanding presence and great authority he told the irritated passengers that our trans-Tasman flight would be at a cruising height of 33 000 feet. At that altitude the wings of an aircraft can ice up and cause dangerous instability to the Boeing 747. The device he was holding was an anti-freezing component, which prevented this potential problem.

It was detected that this component in our aircraft was faulty, and the instrument he was holding was a replacement. It had just been flown in from Melbourne, hence the delay. He went on to say, with great conviction, that it was Qantas policy to put safety first at all times, which is why Qantas has an unblemished world safety record and 'your safety is paramount to the Qantas team that serve you'.

The mood in the terminal changed immediately and there was reserved emotion from all the passengers, including myself; all except for the Texans, however, who stood and applauded, yelling their approval as only the Americans can do. In fact I expected the buggers to start chorusing 'The Yellow Rose of Texas'!

Being a frequent flyer, I am a big fan of Qantas: they do a great job in assisting me to meet my busy speaking schedule. On this occasion, however, their customer service excelled – because of the emotion of the customer connection process. They turned a potential service problem into a memorable experience. We all know that the customer remembers the service, long past the price!

And I still meet customers who remember that memorable day when John Denver came to Toombul ... indeed, 'Some days are diamonds'!

> *If there's a rock 'n' roll heaven ...*
> *well you know they've got a hell of a band.*

> Righteous Brothers 1974

BULLET POINTS

- It's what you do after you do what you're expected to do, that matters most.

- Repeat or referral customers are the most profitable because there are no acquisition costs.

- The customer remembers the service, long past the price!

Chapter 13

Change is not a threat

BULLISM™: CHANGE-A-BULL

Habits reside in the comfort zone of mediocrity.

Barry Bull

Saturation creates evaporation. What you do today can be redundant tomorrow, but some traditions never change. The tradition of good old-fashioned customer service together with a willingness to change to match new market demands is always a winning business combination. I actively look for change and observe with interest the industries that are flourishing by changing simple out-dated business cultures.

The emergence of the café culture in modern society is a good example. The romance of the coffee aroma has blossomed into a love affair of addictive proportions for many lifestyle leisure seekers. In fact, the coffee shop has replaced the office as a meeting place for many busy execs. I must confess that I have always preferred the coffee shop rather than the boardroom for my business meetings.

There are now more coffee shops than ever before, and modern franchise systems have taken the concept of coffee (which once was America's staple beverage) to global superstardom. Starbucks, The Coffee Club and Gloria Jeans are just a few, and competition is fierce to capture a share of society's addiction to caffeine and its love of a good inexpensive social outing, which is the real value of the business as I see it. Astute marketers of coffee understand that the experience and sense of community are of equal importance to the product.

To give credit, however, the coffee business in America was redefined by Starbucks. Some twenty-five years ago, in the halcyon development days of Coke and Pepsi in the US, it was considered that youth didn't want hot beverages and coffee sales plummeted.

Along came Starbucks and took the kitchen culture back to the café culture by introducing some revolutionary changes to a tradition that craved reinvention. They remarketed the category so it had youth appeal: cappuccino, frappuccino, latte, all with gourmet blend, packaged in an environment that romanced the coffee aroma. It became a social experience, and being a hot beverage took time to consume, which provided an opportunity to expand the product offer. The longer a customer stayed the more they spent, so gourmet muffins became a menu must and jazz music was not only the staple mood mellower, but also became part of the experience. Starbucks Jazz CDs were on sale, and tables where you could go on line with your laptop appealed to email and chat-room junkies. Is it any wonder there are now five thousand Starbucks outlets worldwide.

Now before I get into the reasons for why I regularly visit a coffee shop, it needs to be understood that nothing remains the same. Aggressive developers are continually increasing rents for prime locations and every good coffee shop needs a good position. So, like all growth industries, product saturation eventually creates outlet evaporation. While the coffee brand is strong today it won't continue forever. Inevitably it will be challenged by a new 'flavour of the month'. It is easy to see what that will be.

Observe the rapid emergence of the fresh juice business, with clever imaging that promotes lifestyle and health. It is quite obvious with the ageing population and the trend towards alternative lifestyles and healthier diets that the health industry will emerge as one of the world's biggest growth industries this decade. This change in consumer lifestyle has affected two of the most established brands in the world.

Who would have believed that bottled water would become one of the world's biggest selling beverages? Consumers, who once bought soft drinks, now carry a bottle of water because it's healthier, usually cheaper and refillable. Companies like Coca-Cola recognised this trend and to sustain a falling market share of their famous product, entered the bottled water industry. Not surprisingly, the Coca-Cola Company owns and distributes its share of the bottled water we consume. They had to change. They recognised a consumer trend towards a competitive beverage and embraced the change. Not surprisingly, they regained their share of shelf space in refrigerators around the world.

> *The past does not equal the future.*
>
> Anthony Robbins

McDonald's, the world's biggest franchised brand, needed to change to meet the challenge of a health-conscious consumer, so they provided alternative options to their traditional offer. Both Coca-Cola and McDonald's recognised that the past does not equal the future and what you do today can be redundant tomorrow. These two icons of globalisation know that change is inevitable and nothing is forever. By adopting alternative strategies, they discovered that changing markets also expose hidden treasures.

Change is not a threat – it is an opportunity

The survival of the fittest ultimately comes down to one thing – good old customer service. If it is good, it need never change. Mostly, however, this is not the case. To illustrate how customer service can immediately improve business, let me now get back to one of my regular pastimes, socialising in coffee shops.

Queensland's Sunshine Coast where I live is one of Australia's fastest growing regions, with quality resort development attracting national recognition and unprecedented population growth.

Who would have believed that bottled water would become one of the world's biggest selling beverages?

The coffee shops are prolific. One proprietor complained to me recently that his rent had increased twenty per cent. As I was a regular, I told him that the answer to his problem was to simply increase his sales accordingly and explained how he could get an immediate fifty per cent increase in his coffee sales. I informed him that all the times I had been coming to his café for a coffee I was *never* asked if I would like *another* cup of coffee. He was happy for me to use his (expensive) real estate for my social convenience and business meetings for as long as I liked. All for the price of a cup of coffee.

Think about it? How often are you asked if you would like a second cup? Most likely if we are enjoying the company and the occasion we would readily agree to another beverage, or even food. Hence, the sale is doubled. I reckon fifty per cent of patrons would agree with me. They just need to be asked!

Fact file: Recent retail research indicated that seventy per cent of people don't buy because they are not approached.

In essence, what is needed is a willingness to change, deal with the fundamental issues, accept new ideas, react to market conditions, and provide good customer service. In our business, tradition shows that the longer a customer stays in our store, the more they spend. That's retailing, and that's why we are in business. What sets our business apart from our competition, however, is customer service.

The fear of change

While it's natural to resist change it's also in our nature to be fearful. Fear of failure is the number one dream killer, yet fear is a natural condition of human emotions. I wake early each morning and I'm often greeted with negative thoughts. It's strange how the body's chemistry can change during sleep time. I can wake to thoughts of a fear of failure. What if this, what if that; negative thoughts of self doubt that can be quite real and unsettling. Now, I have absolutely no reason to feel a failure as I attribute much of my success to having a positive attitude. Yet whatever fears I have seem to manifest at the beginning of my day. A friend of mine suffers badly from morning depression, so I understand this syndrome is not uncommon.

I deal with this debilitation by disciplining my thinking into positive thoughts of things that please me, and I will go for a walk and take time to value life. As mentioned earlier you need to be in control of everything you think, for a thought remains a thought until it is linked to an emotion. Discipline is necessary to nurture your thoughts and control fear. If I tolerate negative thinking it can become real because what we think about we believe. The good news, however, is the realisation that ninety per cent of our battles with fear are fought with an imaginary foe. They never happen. If the power of the mind can stimulate unfounded fear, it also has the capacity to believe that anything is possible. It all depends on your attitude. And we all have a choice regarding the attitude with which we will embrace each day.

One of the reasons high achievers represent less than ten per cent of the population is because they have learnt the value of change. They know how to embrace it rather than fear it and they realise that the ability to change is governed by the discipline to kick old habits. Habits reside in the comfort zone of mediocrity. It's easier to do nothing. It's always been like this. That's how we always did it. And so on. This attitude, however, becomes an addiction that is eventually hard-wired into our brain and is why people find it difficult to break traditions. This is the challenge – which predictably is my next Bullism.

BULLET POINTS

- Tradition craves reinvention.

- Product saturation eventually creates outlet evaporation.

- The past does not equal the future – what you do today can be redundant tomorrow.

- If the mind can stimulate unfounded fear, it also has the capacity to make you believe anything is possible.

Chapter 14

The challenge of change

BULLISM™: CHALLENGE-A-BULL

Life shrinks or expands according to one's courage.

Dick Sutphen

True success usually resides outside your comfort zone. To get out of your comfort zone is to challenge fear through change. Take a chance. Have the courage to have a go and don't let fear be your dream-killer. Your business only grows as fast as you do. To see change in your business you first need to change yourself. We all have strengths and weaknesses, and the ability to improve our weakness is not only difficult, it first requires the courage to accept that the weakness exists.

It's long been recognised that humans are creatures of habit. We like to follow a trail of familiarity, a daily routine; a journey through a comfort zone with no surprises. Yet change is all around us and what worked in the past won't necessarily work in the future. This is the challenge of change.

You need to change before you have to; take action before you are forced to; reinvent before obsolescence is the only option. Businesses that were challenged by future threats showed courage in modifying traditional business models to fit a new time-poor consumer with different purchasing habits. Pizza Hut closed traditional restaurants and introduced take away and home delivery services, which was in step with new trends introduced by aggressive competition. Sizzler changed its traditional menu and McDonald's added options to theirs to meet a consumer change towards a healthier diet.

The digital challenge

There are no bigger challenges than in my industry, where the global music industry is currently experiencing significant technological change. Direct-to-consumer alternatives challenge the industry's vertically integrated retail distribution model. The internet, peer-to-peer software, MP3s, iPods and other formats have transformed the way music is distributed and enjoyed by consumers. As a consequence, piracy, and illegal downloading on peer to peer networks is also changing the distribution of music and video into a free-for-all feeding frenzy in the traditional food chain. Piracy, online and on the street, continues to plague the music community and its partners in the technology sector. What does the future hold for the music industry, the music stores, independent and major record labels, artists, managers, composers, and publishers in the age of free music downloads and the ubiquitous MP3 file? In fact the number of CDs shipped to retail in the US in 2004 is down twenty-one per cent from 1999 figures and illegal file-sharing has cost the British music industry one billion pounds over the last three years.

A legal and safe electronic distribution method is the desired outcome for everyone in the industry. The survival and prosperity of the industry depends on the copyright owners' ability to protect their intellectual property and maintain a revenue stream that rewards creators. This all needs to be done in the distribution chain whilst maintaining value and convenience to consumers.

This is the challenge of the record companies who undoubtedly will pursue the opportunity of direct-to-consumer digital distribution. This opens up a whole new market as well as creating new revenue streams as broadband penetration evolves.

Shared values

How will traditional retailers remain relevant in an environment where technology is changing consumption habits? Firstly they will need to adapt. To stay in the game, they will realise that physical product will share the market with digital downloads, which end up as a song in a miniature receiving device, such as a mobile phone or an iPod. Competition in the future will be a techno-hungry consumer with a wireless hand-held digital assistant. The content kings and the technology facilitators will be the power brokers of the future.

The challenge to traditional retail is to remain part of this technology integration by being important to suppliers, and relevant and of value to consumers. This will be achieved by specialising in those attributes valued by consumers who prefer established technologies with physical formats and the in-store experience. History continually reminds us that consumers also want emotion in their shopping experience. While technology enhances the convenience of the transaction experience, it won't replace social shopping traditions. Shared values will prevail. Television didn't replace the radio, and cinemas did not close because of video rental. The markets simply expanded. Digital delivery systems won't replace traditional retail, they will coexist. However, 'brick-and-mortar' retailers will need on-line and in-store purchasing options to be of value to their customers.

On-line music is a reality and new consumers will discover new music through this medium even if it means selecting a song not an album. This could be a positive outcome for all participants and encourage new relationships with retailers, providing the content owners include retailers in their digital world. However, *relationship* is the operative word. People will buy on line, but they must be given a reason to buy in-store. Retailers must understand that every contact is a relationship and they can no longer rely for custom on people passing their store. Email, web sites, internet, telephone, referrals and face-to-face are all customer relationships that must be nurtured and valued. This is why our loyalty club is important.

Internet distribution is not the sole reason why global music sales are declining. It needs to be remembered that the CD is a mature format and a twenty-year-old technology. Very few technologies last more than twenty years before their value diminishes.

The long-play microgroove record enjoyed a prosperous twenty-five-year life cycle and is quite likely the format that introduced music into most of our lives. It seemed invincible until the cassette proved to be a more portable and convenient sound carrier. Once the superior digital quality

Technology is changing consumption habits.

of the compact disc was introduced in the mid-eighties, however, both the LP and cassette became redundant in a few short years.

This suited retailers because it was expensive to maintain an inventory of three formats of the same product. This also suited record companies. As LPs and cassettes were replaced by the revolutionary CD format, a new opportunity to remarket catalogue emerged. Consumers embraced the idea of replacing their favourite vinyl albums with this new format. They had little choice because record companies deleted the old format rapidly and the LP was incompatible with the hardware energising the new digital technology.

And so the LP went the way of the seventy-eight and the forty-five single. They were mourned by few because of the sonic quality of digital audio and the robust and portable advantages that the CD provided to consumers on the move. These were the halcyon days of opportunity for the music industry and it enjoyed unprecedented growth and profits. Everybody benefited. This revenue stream rewarded a new breed of talent which gave birth to new music that was eagerly embraced by consumers with an insatiable appetite for entertainment. Everyone in the supply chain was rewarded and benefited from the revenue stream. Although the public had a perception that they were paying too much for their music, Australian CDs were among the cheapest in the world. And still are!! However, that's another story. Importantly the consumer benefited because the industry was prosperous with a comprehensive and immediately available range.

The big difference with on-line music delivery is that technology allows the consumer to dictate the future direction of consumption, not the traditional stakeholders, record companies and artists. Because the internet has provided a platform for free downloads, the music industry cannot recover what is rightfully theirs: the right to revenue from their copyrights. There is no free lunch and until a secure way of supporting the legitimate distribution of music is developed, the consumer will eventually be the one who will be disadvantaged, because no one works for nothing. It needs reminding that file-swapping and downloading from the internet without paying for the product is tantamount to stealing.

Diversification

An answer to this digital dilemma is diversification. Businesses like ours will need to change to be part of this new technology as non-physical product becomes available. The emergence of DVD has provided opportunities for diversification and is the gateway into home cinema technology. This is a division in which we are enjoying strong growth as consumer demand favours an advanced home entertainment experience.

While this technology shift has been taking place, we have been busily leveraging off our core competencies (our CD and DVD business) and seizing opportunities to develop new business. Just as the CD replaced the LP, the DVD has replaced the video (VHS). While there is a window of opportunity to establish our DVD business (before broadband allows this format to go the way of the CD), the DVD and other technologies has opened a whole new treasure chest of home entertainment opportunity. Connectivity solutions for multi-media applications are the next step in the integration of home cinema, music, security, lighting, internet and other technologies for the home. Home networking technology has reached a level where personal computer and consumer electronics vendors can now fully address connectivity for a myriad of devices in the home.

As we diversified into the new opportunities which our industry was pioneering we became more relevant and valuable to our customers by exposing them to the future of home entertainment. We used the technology that was threatening us as an opportunity to put a fresh face to our business. But we were forced to reinvent our business model. And by using the internet as an endless source of information about specialised repertoire, our service value and communication links to our core music customers improved immeasurably.

The challenge of change

While constant change is necessary in business, it is our own individual ability and willingness to change that matters most. Many people find the risks, inflated by fear, overwhelming, and it takes a great deal of personal courage to meet this challenge.

Winston Churchill's profound statement, that 'Kites rise highest against the wind – not with it' assists me whenever life gets tough. I have found that I made the most progress in my life when challenged by opposition and fear. I *had* to change.

Was I scared of change? Do kangaroos poo in the bush? Of course I was! But learning to overcome fear, the biggest dream-killer of all, is the moment when we discover our true potential. When you have a go at the unknown, the doorways of opportunity miraculously open in the most unexpected way. It's knowing that the door is open and stepping through that sends our kite flying highest.

Reinvention is walking through a distant door that is never closed.

Several years ago, I realised that, with my family joining our business and growing into management roles, we would need to expand to support the 'young Bulls'. But this 'old Bull' was reluctant to open more stores. Anyone can get more sales, the trick is to get more profit, and the challenge is to get more people to buy more products using existing assets.

Many will disagree with me here, but I believe that in my industry you don't necessarily make more profit by duplication. To expand the existing brand, without increasing overheads, and maximising existing assets was a smarter option for me. Besides, I wasn't challenged by more of the same. Winning a bunch of awards is great, but there is more to life than past performance. It was time for me to move on and for the family to grow. You have to let go to grow. I yearned for something different. When that 'something different' found me it was so unexpected yet so right. I knew then that my future was to share my experience with others. It's an indulgence I enjoy and I am taking advantage of it right now.

Reinvention

Because Toombul Music had an unbeatable record of winning the major Westfield retail business awards, Westfield invited me to speak to their retailers about the tactics I'd used to gain the success and recognition that won us the awards. They were large forums and I shared the fear of public speaking common to most people. But I enjoyed the experience, and found I had much to offer. Over time I gained the necessary confidence to speak naturally to an audience on a subject about which I am extremely passionate. It didn't take long for the professional speaking bureaus to corral the 'raging Bull', and I was on my way.

It took courage to challenge my fear of reinvention, but by perseverance, I discovered a career direction that was not at all obvious, yet it fitted perfectly with my ambition to build a new business fuelled by my own intellectual property and not burdened by the three business nasties (stock, salaries and rent). At the same time, significant value and reputation were added to our family business. I am now a veteran of over 300 business presentations and have enjoyed the experience of writing. My life has expanded since discovering that change is not a threat, but a remark-a-bull opportunity.

REMARK-A-BULL

Let me put this another way. I don't know about you but I was exhausted just watching the remarkable performances of the old rockers in concert recently. We've seen the best in the past year with The Eagles, John Farnham and Tom Jones, Rod Stewart, Neil Diamond, Cher, Moody Blues and Bette Midler. Now I'm not complaining because I just love their musical performances, being an old sixties rocker myself, but what is even more remarkable is the way in which their music never dies or, more importantly, the way in which these superstars remain relevant to their fans. That's the music biz for you – people love music and I should know because I have made a career of it for over forty years. But I also know that it's the *business* of music that makes the *music business*.

Besides being consummate entertainers, all of these performers are immaculate business people who have a passion for their work. Their performance is not a job, it's a career, and these seasoned entertainers have sustained careers long past their use-by date. Why is this? It's because they love performing, and by consistent recording and touring, they remain relevant to their fans. They keep the dream alive by telling their market that it's okay to relive their youth and enjoy the memories of a time when life was a little less complicated. And their customers keep coming back. If they don't, these remarkable entertainers reinvent themselves and find ways to keep their careers active and their product relevant. If you doubt this then take a look at the aforementioned celebrities. John Farnham partnering with Tom Jones, and Rod Stewart becoming a forties crooner are the most obvious examples.

Now let's use this paradigm in your business. What keeps your customers coming back? What is it that you do that differentiates you from the competition? What do you need to do to remain relevant to your market?

The most important ingredient that makes all the difference is *passion*. And the most important fundamental to remain relevant to your market year after year is the ability to *change and reinvent* yourself. This is the challenge of change. Nothing is forever.

Great businesses succeed because they have someone at the helm who pursues the passion and knows the time when their industry demands change and their business requires reinvention. Sadly, many good businesses of the past have now gone because they lacked this vision. I have been in the music business since 1958, and whilst I admit I have given rock 'n' roll the best years of my life, what's more remark-a-bull is – I still enjoy it! Rolf Harris nailed it when he said, 'Find your obsession, make it your profession and you'll never work another day.'

BULLET POINTS

- Your business only grows as fast as you do.

- To get out of your comfort zone is to challenge fear through change.

- You have to let go to grow.

- Kites rise highest against the wind – not with it.

- Diversify or die.

- Reinvention is walking through a distant door that is never closed.

THE BULLSEYE PRINCIPLE™

5 MEASURE PERFORMANCE

BE GOOD, BE BETTER, BE THE BEST!

Chapter 15

Build a team
– invest in people

BULLISM:™ APPRECI-A-BULL

A person's greatest emotional need is to feel appreciated.

Brian Dyson; CEO Coca–Cola

G reat team leaders understand the importance of appreciating their team. To be a valued part of a team builds personal self-esteem, enhances performance, develops confidence and sustains loyalty. Competent sports coaches understand this, but many business coaches don't.

People are business's biggest asset and its biggest cost. It makes sense to invest in the best asset to attain the biggest result. If you want to achieve your goal of working on your business, not in it, then you'll need a team strategy to do this.

Here is my *Bullseye Principle* for setting up a team strategy. It follows the *good, better, best* model, and allows improvement to be made in stages. If you measure performance in small increments then goals are easier to achieve. The development of a winning team depends on the small changes that are made each day to a person's performance which improve skills and provide personal satisfaction. People start out by being *good* at tasks that provide personal satisfaction and because of this they get *better*. By gaining experience and confidence they can eventually become the *best*. It's a question of measuring individual performance levels so that natural ability is nurtured, skills are developed and improvement is encouraged.

Leadership

Leadership is getting ordinary people to deliver extraordinary results.

Tom Landry, Dallas Cowboys coach

Behind every successful athlete or every winning team is a great coach. The team leader. The same applies in business. But successful team leaders are a rare breed in business because of the misconception that leadership is management. There's a big difference. Businesses succeed because of strong leadership. They fail because of weak management. Top business leaders know that inspiring their team by being close to the action and leading from the front is the best way to implement management policies and procedures. Effective leadership is the most critical component of management because it involves teamwork. And teamwork wins awards. Leadership provides direction, motivation, discipline, good goal focus and lots of training. Lead by example and show the way by your own actions. Don't expect others to give a performance that you are not prepared to give yourself. Remember, winners get what they want by helping others get what they want.

The right people in the right place at the right time

In his book *Good to Great* author Jim Collins says, 'The old adage that people are your most important asset is wrong. People are not your most important asset. The *right* people are.'

Misunderstanding individual core competencies is an easy mistake to make. Misplaced abilities breed problems. Failure to integrate individual skills and competencies into the team mix weakens performance and creates dissatisfaction. For example, if John is better at sales then he should sell. If Sue is better at numbers then finance is for Sue. If Tom is a good organiser then supervision is where Tom will fit best.

As fundamental as this may seem, people are misplaced in organisations if the tasks they are given to do don't suit them, and vice versa. To solve key people problems within your organisation firstly analyse the individual core competencies of your team, then formulate job descriptions around what each does best. Establish assignments and goals around the strengths and weaknesses of your individual team players. One person's strength will support another's weakness. Give your people the right tasks and make sure they integrate with your team objectives. At the same time, however, be sure that the team objectives match your business objectives.

You can't assign tasks unless you understand where each team member excels. The best way to do this is to *ask them*! Find out what they like doing because that's the job they are going to do best. *Good* people get *better* because they achieve satisfaction from their work. With the right nurturing they become your *best* employees. We can't all be good at everything, but we do need to be good at the right things. We are usually good at doing things we like. We've all heard the saying 'a square peg in a round hole'. Incompatibility eventually breeds failure in most things in life; this is especially so in business. By placing the right people in the right place at the right time you are sure to achieve the best result.

Assigning people to perform tasks that don't suit their talents or ability is a wasted effort. Human nature is hard to change and it is difficult to challenge instinctive behaviour. The time to determine a person's suitability is in the interviewing process while recruiting. Have a job description available so interviewees clearly understand the job on offer and if you ask the right questions you will determine their suitability.

Just as listening is important in selling it's also essential in training. Listening is the key to good team development because good listeners make informed communicators.

The back-up buddy

Everyone performs best with the comfort and support of others. For the best team result I have always assigned each team player a 'buddy' for support. It's the first rule of team building: support each other so everyone shares the benefits of the teamwork. The 'buddy' system provides important back-up to each team member, as well as creating team partnering, which provides mutual support during busy periods. I find our team is strongest when each member has the comfort and support of a back-up buddy.

*Assigning people to perform tasks that don't suit their talents
or ability is a wasted effort.*

Training

Courage and confidence come with knowledge and training.

My colleague, Tom O'Toole, the Baker from Beechworth in Victoria, is a good retailer and he has a good rule on training. When people ask him, 'What if I train them and they leave?' Tom's reply is, 'What if I don't and they stay?'

Communication is vital to team building and making sure everyone understands the team objectives. There are two ways to effective team training: group, and one-on-one. In group training I target the two 'P's – Product and Policy. My goal here is to provide product knowledge and maintain procedural disciplines. The reason group training can't be totally successful is because it deals with general issues and fails to solve individual performance criteria.

One-on-one training is needed to reinforce the objectives, to personalise the problems and to acknowledge effort and encourage growth. One-on-one performance evaluation is also essential. This is where good people get better.

We have twenty key people in our organisation and every morning it has been my practice to take one of the team to the nearby coffee shop between nine and ten. Why this time? Simple. Humanity seems to need a caffeine fix at this time of the day and because of this we feel relaxed, refreshed and receptive to performance discussion. I also do this early when people are fresh and never do it in the office because it's too formal and prone to interruptions. Offices can be dangerous places, so for that reason I don't spend much time in mine.

Measurement and reward

I review performance, formalise procedures, discipline, solve problems and reward results. I listen to the team member's response and am able to review performance against the job description. This procedure requires uninterrupted quality time, and a management attitude that tends towards assisting *good* people to improve and to achieve a *better* level of personal satisfaction in their work. This encourages their *best* efforts.

This is effective leadership and the presence or lack of it is mostly why management succeeds or fails. If the same message and motivation are coming from the top, then the whole team has a clear understanding of the direction in which they are heading. This also ensures that your team goals are consistent with the goals of your business.

This is why I love the challenge of small business. I went into business *for* myself but not to be *by* myself. This activity allows me the opportunity to impress our company's vision on each member of our team. Admittedly it takes time, but it's time well spent. Your people are worth it; they are the biggest cost to most businesses. It makes sense to focus on and value your biggest investment. I find that quality time with quality people provides a quality result.

Needs and wants

There are two important things that influence people to perform: their *needs* and their *wants*. Our needs in life include essentials such as food and water, shelter, good health and the need to be loved. As long as we have them we will survive. We need money to achieve these. But life becomes dull unless we put some *wants* into it: some fun, joy, entertainment and material possessions. These also take money. It's a question of how much money is needed to achieve the needs and wants. It's knowing the difference. *Wants* we can do without, *needs* we can't. The key is getting the right balance. Wealth is what most desire but there are a lot of wealthy people who are unhappy because they don't have their needs and wants in perspective. Conversely, wants can dominate other people's needs because of greed or an obsession with material possessions they can't really afford. This same balance is essential in the effective management of people. It's critical that management understands the *needs* and *wants* of their team. People want to be paid for what they're worth, however, they don't just work for money. They also want job satisfaction, recognition and advancement opportunity. These are all important components to employee loyalty and the balance is to get it right.

One of management's greatest failings is to not tell its people that they are appreciated. Sometimes the smallest of rewards, like *thank you*, give the biggest result. If you're doing well – *reward them*! If they're doing well – *tell them*!

BULLET POINTS

- Put the right people in the right place at the right time.

- Be sure that the team objectives match the business objectives.

- Good listeners make informed communicators.

- Courage and confidence come with knowledge and training.

- Quality time with quality people provides a quality result.

- *Wants* we can do without, *needs* can't be compromised.

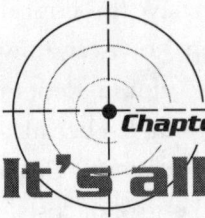

Chapter 16

It's all about efficiency

BULLISM™ SIZE-A-BULL

Size works against excellence.

Bill Gates

Costs are the enemy

Downsizing is not a dirty word – it's all about efficiency. As our business grew, so did our space and stock, until one day our overheads became an uncomfortable burden to carry. Although turnover was increasing, profit wasn't commensurate with sales growth.

Business today is burdened by rising costs. Annual rent and wages increases, and pressured margins due to increased competition, are the biggest challenges to the bottom line. Only by making mandatory checks on profit performance, by regular analysis of income and expenses, can profit budgets be achieved. One of the important checks and balances for me is the monitoring of acceptable rent to turnover percentage.

Fixed costs are a fact of life and, apart from wages, rent is usually the biggest business expense. Rent as a percentage of turnover is a key factor in determining how much rent a business can afford to pay. This calculation is based on the business's gross profit. As a rule of thumb (depending on the industry) a retail business with a gross profit of thirty-three per cent should pay a maximum of five to six per cent of turnover in rent. I know of some that pay well in excess of ten per cent! Franchise businesses have this critical calculation built into their business model. It is surprising, however, how many independent businesses are ignorant of this simple formula. Rent to turnover percentage has always been on top of my business hit list because it is surprising how creeping costs can really hurt in the long term. Costs are the enemy. Efficiency in business demands continual control of costs.

Reassess the requirement

As we approached the end of our last lease period, it was clear that the business couldn't continue the way it had operated for the past twenty years. The rent to turnover percentage was growing at an unacceptable rate, which can happen so easily over the term of a lease. It was the biggest road block to achieving our future profit aspirations.

Fact file: Rent is like a migrating bird, it heads north annually.

We took radical but necessary action and I renegotiated my new lease with downsizing in mind. Due to the shape of our store and its corner location, I surrendered twenty-five per cent of the back end of our premises. By reducing our space by a quarter the rent fell accordingly. It should be noted that your best sales areas will always remain the true front of the shop, the area next to the main pedestrian flow. So even though I gave up twenty-five per cent of the space, I wasn't giving up twenty-five per cent of the traffic flow. It was always difficult to attract customers through the entire store and the decision to lose space at the rear had many productivity implications.

I then analysed our considerable stockholding and by applying the eighty-twenty principle (eighty per cent of sales come from twenty per cent of inventory), I prudently reduced inventory. I concentrated on stock depth not stock width, for example, never being out of good sellers but eliminating unproductive slow movers.

That was over a year ago and our sales were not dramatically affected but our profit returned to healthy levels. Even with one store (albeit a big one), big is not necessarily best, but by concentrating on being more efficient, our profit became the best in years. Timely downsizing made our three biggest blockbuster expenses – wages, rent and inventory – more efficient. By skilfully maintaining turnover we had capital for other things. Nowadays I do not reinvest in inflating my stock, but quite the opposite. By keeping a close watch on the efficiency of my asset, I invest to improve the efficiency of other growth assets, like the good ol' super fund.

Negotiating the lease

When you are operating a business in premises you do not own, it is critical that rent negotiation is viewed as one of the most important you will enter into. Big business has definite advantages over smaller businesses when negotiating rental rates with landlords. Achieving reasonable and fair rent deals has to be the objective of anyone serious about attaining the right levels of return on business investment. It is a game of skill, tenacity and an understanding of the negotiation process. Mostly it's reaching an agreement that is acceptable to both the lessor and the lessee. The following are some helpful guidelines in understanding the rules when lease negotiation time arrives.

1. Plan the negotiation

When renegotiating your lease in a major shopping centre, plan the process at least twelve months before renewal time. Many landlords prepare their revenue budgets at least twelve months in advance, which is standard budgeting practice. Once cash flow and asset values are determined the budgets are approved by management, and these financial estimates form the business plan that determines future rental rates. As you know, landlords don't come and discuss future rents to be budgeted for your premises. They have different financial objectives to what we operators have. If you find out their budgeting cycle then you can plan for this. If you wait until the expiry of the lease there is little room to negotiate. You have a livelihood to protect and it can be a mistake to leave the tenure of your premises to the last minute. If you have a successful business, you have no choice but to agree to rents that may be unreasonable, if you leave no time on the lease.

It is the landlord's responsibility to achieve as high a rental return as the market will pay (within reason) and therefore a late negotiation tends to be in the landlord's favour. If you have a tenancy issue then you need to discuss this with your landlord before new rental structures are set. This is what I did. To get a reasonable result it is advisable to do these things well before lease expiry, using the principles I outline here.

2. The term of the lease
It is important to budget your break-even sales figure for each year of the lease term. You need sales forecasts to cover overheads at the beginning of the lease term and at the end. Once you have signed a lease you are locked in and the rent will be the lowest at this point of your new lease term. The compounding effect of annual increases, such as CPI and operating costs, requires an annually budgeted sales and profit performance to cover these incremental increases over the term of the lease. When you negotiate a new lease you must know your break-even sales to cover rent at the *expiry* of the lease. If the lease term is five years then the question you must ask is: 'Can you afford to pay the rent in five years' time?' This is where the five-year business plan is critical. Look for options on the lease and ways to limit the amount of increase that the landlord can impose.

3. Think beyond the term of the lease
Once the lease term matures, rent usually rises on the next renewal. Owners are always seeking bigger returns on their investment. With fixtures and fittings and other capital investments it is not easy to walk away. You need to think beyond the term of the lease because most businesses are long term. Significant capital is invested at the start of a lease with expensive legal and fit-out costs. Where your business is long term, negotiating longer-term (rather than short-term) leases allows fixtures and fittings to be depreciated over the term of the lease. Be aware that some owners will require you to completely replace fittings or totally refurbish the tenancy every time you enter into a new lease. Also some leases require expensive make-good conditions if the tenancy is vacated. This will apply whether the

lease is short term or longer term. You need to be aware of these conditions. Businesses with long leases are much easier to sell. Security of tenure is an important criterion to someone buying a business.

Like everything in business it takes strength and knowledge to make long-term decisions.

4. Big is not always best

Being in the biggest centre doesn't always mean you'll succeed, just as some parts of a street are good and others are not. The cost of opening a store in a big centre can be much higher than in smaller centres due to fit-out demands. Although the expectations are high, so are the rents and the fall can be the greatest from the big regional centres. Bankruptcy is not far away if you get it wrong.

While position is everything in retailing it also needs to be affordable. Success in business depends on the continual analysis of the cost of customer acquisition. Choose a location or a shopping centre where the competition is weak and where you can dominate your market category. This enables you to be of value to the centre and businesses of value are the ones that can get the fairest rent deals.

5. What you start out with may not be what you finish with

One thing you must always remember is that the shopping centre industry is always changing. Make sure you ask as many questions as you can about the landlord's intentions on tenancy mix and renovations. Today, there is considerable protection afforded by legislation for the small shop operator. However, most centres regularly change in format and mix. You need to feel assured that the position you choose at the start of the lease does not suffer from fundamental changes in the design and layout of the centre over time. This can take many forms, such as major tenancy failure, planned new access points, the introduction of cinemas or other uses that compete for prime car-parking space. If you think this is an exaggeration, let me remind you of the restructuring that took place with Harris Scarfe

Stores, Franklins Supermarkets and Daimaru Department Stores. All these greatly affected small shop performance during these difficult times. This is a complex area and leads me to the next point.

6. Seek professional advice

Do the due diligence and seek professional advice. Failing to seek the right advice at the beginning is false economy for small business. Factors like occupancy benchmarking (determining average market rent for precinct), rent to sales ratio (as discussed earlier), customer demographic, location, and competition, are all important considerations that must be carefully examined. The right advice can help even up the odds against an experienced leasing agent whose sole purpose is to get you to sign the lease. When you remind yourself that their job is over at that time and your job is only beginning, it helps to clarify why professional assistance is critical. You have one shot at a viable business. Don't blow it by poor negotiations before you even start.

7. Build relationships

It is also important to remember that there is usually no guarantee of an automatic renewal of your lease. Therefore it is important to develop a strong relationship with your landlord so that your position in the tenancy mix is valued. If you are in a shopping centre then regular meetings with centre management are helpful for long-term relationship building. This not only builds trust but allows for the planning of future growth opportunities. Most landlords are cognisant of the long-term value of a stable lessor–lessee relationship. The harsh reality of renting business premises, however, is that some owners' sole objective is to take as much profit from the lessee as possible. They squeeze all the juice from the orange so all that is left is the pip. To avoid these pitfalls, good communication with your landlord is critical and due diligence over the considerations we've discussed is essential before entering into any lease negotiation.

Westfield was our landlord for over twenty years and I rarely came into conflict with them. It was a business partnership that was mutually valued.

In many cases I pushed them instead of them pushing me. My relationship building was so intense, that within a ten-year period most people in the entire Westfield organisation, through to the chairman Frank Lowy, knew our business. It was their business to know our business. It was our business to know theirs. It's called effective partnering. Centro Properties now own Toombul and within two weeks of the ownership change all senior management in Centro knew the value of our business!

Now I can sense a touch of cynicism and doubt here, am I right? You're thinking, 'You've got to be joking, Barry – creating a good relationship with my landlord?' Well, if you're thinking this then you've got some work to do.

One of the most important people in your business relationships is your landlord because they own the premises that support your livelihood. If you add value to their business and have the capacity to pay the rent, then they will want you to stay. A proven relationship that sustains respect and adds value is the best way to negotiate fair lease renewals. This is what I mean.

In July 2003, Westfield sold Toombul Shoppingtown to Centro Properties. The day after this surprise public announcement, I received a call from Westfield managing director Steven Lowy, to personally inform me of the sale. The real purpose of the call was to thank me for the contribution that I had made to their Toombul centre over a long period of time. As the partnership had come to an end this was a nice gesture on Steven's behalf to acknowledge the mutual value of our business dealings. The fact that I received an acknowledgement at all was a most unexpected surprise. But wait – there's more! Three months later Steven was in Queensland inspecting a new Westfield centre that had just opened. On the way to the airport he paid me a personal visit at Toombul. Accompanied by a battalion of troops, the commander-in-chief came to personally say farewell and thank me for our efforts on behalf of the Lowy family. Naturally I was chuffed.

It is a known fact that over a ten-year period, Toombul Music won more Westfield awards than any other Australian retailer. We gave the awards program a real hammering and once we were on a roll there was no stopping us! At the same time we successfully leveraged off those achievements to

Another important business partner to us is our bank manager.

gain significant national recognition for our business. Because we had their respect we were always able to get a hearing at important times. But Steven Lowy's personal visit was more rewarding to me than any of those awards. It showed me the value of true respect. This is the biggest reward you can earn. Our consistent long-term performance had been truly measured that day.

Another important business partner to us is our bank manager. We have been with the same banking institution for almost twenty-five years. They assisted us to build our business, buy our investment properties, our home and our children's homes. As I said earlier I am *big* on loyalty. You must show it if you expect it in return. Loyalty is earned and cannot be bought. Twice yearly I have business meetings with our bank manager to inform him of our progress and provide current financial statements. I keep him totally informed of our financial stability and future growth requirements. I inform him of our twelve-month business plan and the positives and negatives in our business that may influence future financing needs.

It's about prioritising, valuing and nurturing relationships, and making sure that important business partners are on the Christmas card list.

BULLET POINTS

- Measure performance – what gets measured gets done.

- Strength and knowledge are needed when making long-term decisions.

- Success in business is the continual analysis of the cost of acquiring customers.

- Nurture business partnerships and build long-term relationships.

Chapter 17
Time and leverage

BULLISM:™ LEVERAGE-A-BULL

A planned outcome guarantees the best income.

Barry Bull

Time and leverage are powerful partners. If the words *time* and *leverage* are combined, you have the formula for long-term success in most of life's endeavours. *Time* is life, and how we leverage off life's opportunities is the key to prosperity. Some put the time to good use while others are not so fortunate. It's easy to look back on life with regrets for missed opportunities but the future holds the key to redemption, not the past. The successful have learned how to leverage resources like people, money, stocks, and equity to build wealth and prosperity. Over time, the compounding effect of these investments provide for the golden years of retirement.

Research shows that the average Australian will be in retirement for around twenty-five years. The same statistics also reveal that only five per cent will be financially independent by the retirement age of sixty-five. Wealth creation throughout a working career needs to be a fundamental component of any business plan. It is scary how many fail to plan for their future golden years, as the statistics illustrate. The top five per cent share a common way of thinking which is what separates them from the remaining ninety-five per cent. They are focussed on financial freedom and think and act differently from others. That is why they are wealth creators.

The two commonly accepted ways to create wealth are by people working or money working. True wealth is created by leveraging off the efforts of others, or leveraging off capital.

People at work

If you work for the boss then your efforts are being used to provide wealth for someone else and you are trading your time in return for their dollars. In other words someone else is leveraging off your efforts to create financial gain. There is nothing wrong with this because *they* are taking the investment risk. If you are self-employed, own your own business and employ a well-trained team of people, then you are effectively leveraging off their efforts to create financial gain for your business. Owning my own business enabled me to do this – and eventually much more.

For the first few years I concentrated on creating a business model that worked. Initially, I found it easier to do things myself, rather than get others to do them. As the business grew, however, I realised that by investing in others I could get more important tasks done. By building a team of competent and reliable people, we were able to develop a regular clientele that kept growing.

> *Wealth is hidden from those who want to do it all themselves.*
> *Wealth exposes itself to those patient enough to train others.*
>
> Anon.

Eventually I was able to step back from the day-to-day selling and concentrate on management and marketing. This allowed me time to develop leadership skills to sell my ideas to employees, suppliers, our landlord, and carefully targeted consumer markets. It was at this stage that our business grew rapidly. After all, retailing is the process of buying and selling goods and services to create a profit. Like the stock market, the price you pay for your investment determines your return on investment. Business is the same as the stock market; it involves taking risks, implementing diversified strategies to spread the risk and not put all your eggs in one basket.

Diversify or die

If you think that having one store in a single location is putting all your eggs in the one basket, you are absolutely right. But what was also right, was diversifying to hedge against risk. By diversifying our product range and investing whatever we could afford in a wealth creation portfolio (superannuation), we spread our exposure over many investments to minimise risk. By leveraging off the one business we then created two investment portfolios that were independent of each other. This was comfortable for us because we minimised the risk of duplication, which meant opening more stores with more of the same heavy inventories, rents and salaries. Leveraging off one set of overheads in a location that was always within our control was a smarter option for us. At the same time I committed myself to building a nest egg outside the main nest: a superannuation wealth creation portfolio.

At no stage, however, was I ever in a comfort zone. To succeed in an independent enterprise such as a family business, you'd better believe there is no comfort zone. And at no stage was I ever without the thought of failure. Many of you who share my journey would know what I mean. You just get in and work your butt off!

Fear of failure is a natural human instinct. It is the reason people don't take risks and is the true decider between mediocrity and success. Many people from my generation, whose parents struggled to make ends meet, are continually faced with the fear of not ever having enough. Yet they lack the courage to have a go. It was only when I began to understand that risk and fear are artificial barriers that can be broken by good research, strong mentoring and a positive attitude to have a go, that I made real progress toward financial security. My ambitions became greater than my fears.

Money at work

To create wealth you need a business or an income in which to create leverage. In our case we owned our own business. During our early years, all of our profits were reinvested in the business. We leveraged off core competencies to develop other businesses within the brand. When the government introduced compulsory superannuation in 1992, they did us

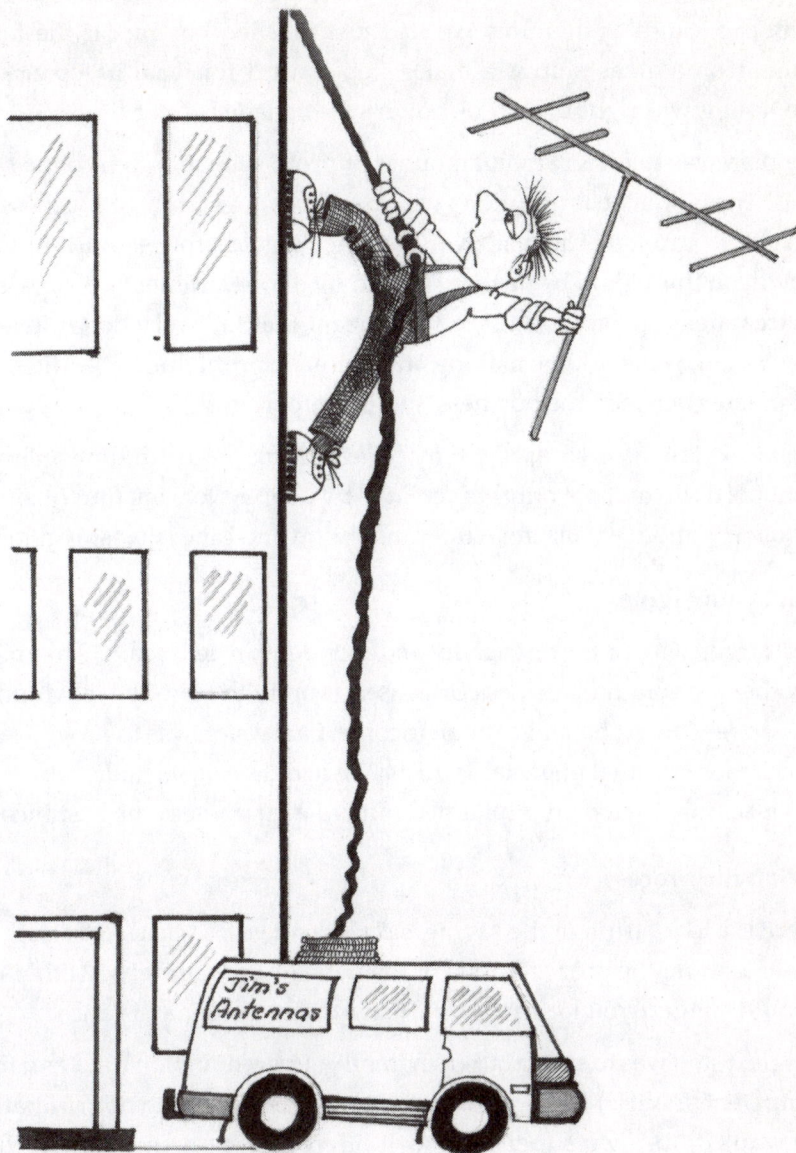

You'd better believe there is no comfort zone in your own business!

a big favour. They forced us to save. I understood the benefits of forced savings because at this time we had just finished paying off the family home. Home ownership is a major step toward financial independence. The timing was right to start our own self-managed super fund.

The plan was to direct small amounts of profit each month into the super fund. These small contributions would not be missed by the business and yet, with compound interest, over time they would grow significantly. The growth on this would be further assisted by the government's concessional tax treatment on super funds, which meant that for every dollar invested in our fund, we would be making an automatic profit due to the difference in tax rates between the business and the super fund.

Let me explain how we applied my *Bullseye Principle* to building an investment portfolio that not only was created by people working (our business), but also by money working (superannuation and other investments).

1. Set your sights

Our target was to be financially independent in ten years. This meant whether we sold the business or passed it on to the family we would not have to rely on the business for an income. Our vision was to progressively provide for eventual financial security. We had time on our side, however, it was also time for a plan. A planned outcome guarantees the best income.

2. Plan the process

There is a lot of truth in the saying, *People don't plan to fail ... they just fail to plan.* Planning the process is one of the most important steps. At this stage I would suggest you look to your financial advisor for assistance.

Our next step was to set up our own family superannuation fund and find a competent financial advisor. Our accountant assisted with both initiatives. We wanted our own super fund as it offered us more investment choice and better control of our investment strategy.

With the ageing population in Australia, the government is obviously very keen to ensure that everyone provides adequate funds for their retirement. One of the ways to encourage individuals to do this is to provide them with generous tax incentives. Once this was fully explained to us we were able to grasp the full potential of how superannuation could help us achieve our target.

The planning process firstly involved looking at how much money we needed for retirement in ten years. Once our goal was targeted and the big picture was clear we worked back from this point. By providing my advisor with a monthly figure in today's dollar terms, he was then able to adjust this for inflation and calculate an accurate amount for what we required as a lump sum. Once we knew this target, it was then simply a process of calculating out how much we needed to set aside on a monthly basis to achieve this target. This proved to be a good decision because the business never missed this regular investment withdrawal. This supports my thinking that small changes regularly are far less disruptive and much more effective than big changes that are made at times of necessity. There's a big difference. Do you know what that difference is? It's having a plan.

3. Implement the strategy

The investment strategy was to develop a diversified portfolio of growth assets of property and shares. Our advisor recommended a broad range of investments including direct shares and managed funds. In our case we already had good exposure to direct property through investment in our home as well as a beach apartment. It was therefore decided to diversify into industrial and commercial property via some property trusts.

It is well understood that higher returns on investment generally mean higher risk and that all investment markets do fall at some time. With an investment time frame of potentially over twenty-five years – ten years leading up to retirement and fifteen years after retirement – it was wise to have predominantly a mixture of growth assets in the lead up to retirement. Then as retirement approaches, the investment strategy would slowly shift from growth to combine income and growth. The aim at retirement was to generate sufficient income to adequately fund our family's needs and wants. In addition, we needed some growth to counter the eroding effects of inflation on our accumulated capital.

4. Deal with the issues

It took time to get comfortable with the fact that our money was being managed by others. Each time the markets dipped we reacted to downturns just like any other investor would. By having a diversified portfolio of shares and property we soon discovered that both these markets worked in opposite cycles to each other. And so we learned to ride the dips and peaks.

Markets tend to run in cycles and often behave totally irrationally. Many people tend to buy property and shares at the top of each cycle and then after two or three years' of disappointing returns, sell at the bottom.

To hit the Bullseye you have to stick to your original strategy and ride out the difficult times. One valuable strategy we learned was to 'Dollar Cost Average' into investment markets. What this means is buying more in a falling market. So rather than investing $5000 by buying 500 shares for $10 each, you buy 100 shares for $10 now, a month later you buy 125 shares at $8 in a falling market, 200 shares at $5 a month later, 125 the next month at $8 and finally 100 shares at the same price of $10 that you originally paid. In this way, you have still invested the same $5000, however by spreading this investment over a number of months the average price you have paid for these shares is $7.70. Once the price reaches the original price of $10 then you would have made a profit of $1500.

5. Measure performance

Every six months my advisor and I measure the performance of each stock or managed portfolio he recommended to me. In addition, we also measure how the portfolio is going against the required targets we set up initially; and together we fine-tune the investment strategy to match our changing circumstances. Managing my cash flow was also critical to my success. As any business owner well knows, the cash flow generated by the business can change very quickly. It was therefore very important to review and adjust amounts invested, investigate any new investment options and re-balance existing investments where necessary.

While superannuation is important, what's equally important is to hedge against legislative changes in this highly regulated area and to diversify into other investments to reduce risk. How you diversify depends on your age and stage of income and family responsibilities. However, the older you get, and as your wealth grows, the more you should diversify to reduce risk.

6. Be disciplined and determined

Just as we had paid off our business loans and our home, the discipline of regular budgeting began to build investments that capitalised over time through compounding interest. There are two types of interest: simple interest – interest paid on principal; and compounding interest – interest paid on principal *and* interest.

Compounding interest is one of the most basic, yet least understood principles of investment. Compounding simply refers to the re-investment of earnings on an investment as you receive them. In other words, interest paid on interest. The growth rate of an investment can accelerate rapidly the longer the funds stay invested.

Fact file: If you invest $11 000 at age twenty then another $3000 each year till age sixty-five (at 7.5 per cent per annum return) it would be worth over $1 000 000. If you started just ten years later at age thirty, however, it would only be worth approximately half that amount.

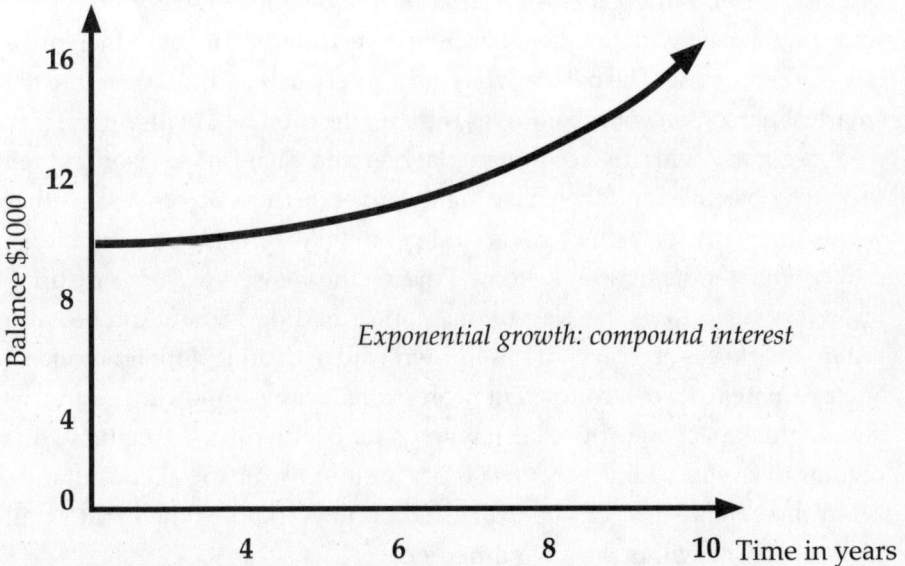

Exponential growth: compound interest

As you can see by the chart, money invested grows exponentially over time as the interest earned on the original investment compounds on itself.

Having a disciplined approach to investment is certainly not easy and there were many times when I was tempted to stray, especially when, for some considerable period of time in 2002–03, share markets slumped and our portfolio lost valuable momentum. Bear markets dominated and the Bull was nowhere to be seen.

Bugger! How I hate market downturns. Negative growth is like *a red rag to a Bull* to me.

Just when many nervous investors were leaving the share market and looking to buy more real estate, our long-term plan called for 'buying low' and 'selling high'. So instead of selling shares at this time, we were busily adding to our portfolio. Shares bought during the slump are now showing the greatest gains in our portfolio.

You can tell how I rely on professional advice from my financial advisor. We need others around us for support and should continually reassess our strengths and weaknesses.

My task is to build businesses, and you can't be good at everything. Surrounding myself with people whose skills are different or better than mine has worked for me. The person who said, 'You're in big trouble if you're the smartest person on your team,' was right on the money! My discipline is to meet regularly with my accountant, lawyer and financial advisor and tell them my objectives and then have them deliver on those objectives. In other words make my goals their goals, and get them to educate us on matters I don't understand, but need to know. Finding the answers to things we don't know, yet need to, is the way to make informed decisions. And because today's market is merciless, it has its own way of dealing with ignorance. I am fortunate to have a competent professional team supporting us and, as you might expect, they have been with us for a long time. To maintain this regular discipline, I budget $10 000 per annum for financial consultancy. I find the benefits exceed the expense. You never know when that small piece of advice will make a big difference.

7. Hit the Bullseye

To reap the rewards of a lifelong active career is to achieve financial freedom upon retirement. Regrettably, this will be a pipe dream for many Australians. Indications are that the current nine per cent compulsory superannuation contributions will only provide a modest standard of living at retirement – particularly for those 'baby boomers' who have only been exposed to the compulsory superannuation guarantee in the latter part of their working lives. While this contribution will raise retirement income well above pension levels, many retirees will experience lower living standards after retirement than before it.

> **Fact file**: Seventy-nine per cent of Australians over the age of sixty-five receive some public pension and sixty-eight per cent of these receive the full pension (FACS survey 2001). The average annual personal income of a full-time Australian worker aged fifty to sixty-nine is $52 500 (Canberra University based National Centre of Social and Economic Modelling). This compares with the average annual personal income of $16 600 for an Australian of the same age who is not in the work force.

This is where *The Bullseye Principle* worked for us. We not only achieved the financial goal we had set our sights on way back in 1992, but gained much more. By understanding the balance between the *bull and bear* cycle in life, true wealth emerged. And it had nothing to do with money. What I mean by this is, by balancing business values with family values, love and happiness prevailed.

But what is balance? It took me a long time to realise that it's a lifelong lesson of understanding values and putting them into perspective.What's important and what's not. It's about disciplining ourselves to deal with success and failure, acceptance and rejection, what's possible and what's not – and knowing the difference.The real value of wealth is not a financial outcome. It's learning how to value life itself.

The Beatles classic, 'Money Can't Buy Me Love', rattles 'round regularly in my brain, because apart from containing a memorable melody the song has a profound lyric. You can't buy love or happiness. They're a state of being, a condition of the soul. As long as wealth doesn't possess us and we possess it, then financial freedom allows us to spend the best years of our life doing the things that make us happy with the ones we love.

It's always important to realise that the road to financial freedom is paved with potholes of personal indulgence. The biggest battle to hit the Bullseye will always be fought with ourselves. On the one hand we want to provide for the future and on the other we live for today. Society seems to judge us on material possessions. Yet if we live beyond our means today, then an aged pension may be our means to an end tomorrow.

Most people don't plan to be on an age pension when they retire. Very few, however, manage to achieve a comfortable retirement after forty years or more in the workforce. I suspect that the reason for this is due to a lack of proper planning. Hitting the Bullseye does not happen by accident. It involves careful thought, good preparation, the right advice and lots of discipline and determination to hit the target.

Time is critical in building retirement income

Whatever your investment strategy happens to be, *time* is the one factor that determines success or otherwise. The time you enter the market and the time you exit is important to wealth creation, but not as important as making the decision to get into the market in the first place. My advisor tells me it's more about *time in* than *timing*. How you then use this time to make the most of opportunities is the key. You can now see why the combination of *time* and *leverage* is the formula for long-term success. Use time wisely to leverage off life's opportunities.

If you want to join the five per cent that achieve financial security then there is no time like *now* to seriously consider if your plan for the future is secure. To determine this you need to answer the questions that I asked at the beginning of this book.

- Where are you now?

- Where do you want to be in the next five years and beyond?

- What is your plan to get there?
- What is your strategy to achieve this?

Time and leverage are powerful partners

It is important to see the big picture, which is what I have endeavoured to paint in this Bullism. By using our own example of wealth creation you can see that we needed to start at the end and work back. We needed to see the big picture. Once we had the goal of financial freedom, hitting the eventual Bullseye was not so daunting. By leveraging off physical and financial resources time became the only factor in hitting our financial goal. This is why I believe that time and leverage are powerful partners.

BULLET POINTS

- Use time to leverage off life's opportunities.
- The future holds the key to redemption, not the past.
- People don't plan to fail ... they just fail to plan.
- You're in big trouble if you're the smartest person on your team.
- The road to financial freedom is paved with potholes of personal indulgence.
- The real value of wealth is not a financial outcome – it's learning how to value life itself.

Chapter 18

The independence of your business

BULLISM: INDEPEND-A-BULL

Progress begins when you accept ownership of your own destiny.

Anon.

I know what you're thinking. There is no such word as *independable*. True. I couldn't find it in the dictionary either. Which is why I have used it. It's one of my favourite Bullisms. It's just another way to make my point. I thrive on the independence of owning the decisions that I make in my own business, and the career rewards that individuality and independence bring. This is my *Bullism* for independence.

Your dream is about you and the life you want to live. It does not have to be significant in the eyes of others but if you find comfort and satisfaction in your life then others will respond to your success. My whole life has been underpinned by the realisation that it doesn't matter what others think. It doesn't matter what others do. What matters is taking action on what's real to me. What's right for me at a particular time and place in my life. This is my independence. By choosing to be an independent retailer I unwittingly chose to accept ownership of my own destiny. So independ-a-bull, with its overtones of independence, is the best word to describe this freedom. But the dictionary says this word doesn't exist? Nor does freedom – unless you make it yourself.

This is an important Bullism for me because it deals with the three things we all seek in life: *good* health, *better* wealth and the *best* lifestyle. Independence allowed me to eventually achieve this, but like all treasures its whereabouts took quite a while to uncover.

The journey so far

Fear is the biggest inhibitor of progress. Being told as a young schoolboy that I wouldn't amount to much unless I improved my marks was teaching *by* fear. These educators were purposely instilling fear as a way of encouraging achievement. What I needed at the time was to be taught self-confidence and self-esteem, not fear of failure. It took me a long time to understand the difference. The prejudices of childhood are a burden that some carry all of their lives. Only by fate putting me in the right place at the right time so that I could discover a career in music did I realise that ambition is the cure for fear.

I have never placed wealth above family. I always wanted my children to grow up nice people and they have. I give a lot of this credit to Kayleen, who has always been the wind beneath our wings. I realised when challenged years ago by an uncompromising and time-demanding corporate career, that *real* wealth is the successful balancing of family and business values. So I changed occupations and became my own boss. This provided the freedom to control my destiny and march to the beat of my own drum, a decision that has served me well over the last two decades. Although I didn't end up marching. Instead I was rockin' to the retail beat of music marketing.

Moving out of the corporate comfort zone into private enterprise was a culture shock. I only adjusted to it when I decided that I wasn't buying myself a job, but creating a new career with one important difference – I was in control.

I didn't have much money after buying our business in 1981, but I had knowledge, and knowledge is power. Thankfully my thirteen-year career working in a high-powered marketing position with one of the world's largest record companies had taught me heaps. During that time the rules for music marketing were just being written, and 'sex, drugs and rock 'n' roll' was an anthem for many in the industry. In the end, I was burnt out, disillusioned, and had had enough. Fortunately, I wasn't brain dead. In fact, I was more like a loaded gun with a chamber of new ideas just waiting to be fired. I had my sights set on a new target. So began the challenging journey of building our own business. The crossing of new retail frontiers has been rewarding to say the least.

I was determined never again to put myself in a position where someone else controlled my time, where I traded my time for their dollars. Mostly for their benefit. Instead, my priority was to spend time with my family and to pursue new business dreams. This was a period of extreme change.

Through continual improvement and the willing introduction of uniqueness and change, we built a successful business with one set of overheads. But the ability to diversify and leverage off our brand has always provided our biggest differentiating advantage.

Work smarter not harder

Jack Collis is a highly regarded business speaker and author of several books, his most renowned bestseller being *Work Smarter Not Harder*. Over the years, Jack and I became friends. We often shared the same stage at business presentations and our commitment to best business practices is a shared passion. He advocates that by working smarter not harder, you allow yourself time to recognise opportunities and to be more efficient with time management. The 'E Myth theory' advocates the same idea, 'work on your business not in it'. I took this good advice, and about ten years ago got out from behind the counter. I never went back. I employed talented people to do the selling for me, while I concentrated on management and marketing. This gave me time to recognise threats and seize opportunities. This freedom also allowed me to understand our customers' needs. I recall sitting on the customer bench in the mall outside our store for thirty minutes each day studying our customers' purchasing habits and looking at our business through their eyes. This was a real eye opener. I adopted the mindset that every customer was visiting our store for the first time; I trained my team to write down all the products they were asked for that we didn't stock, which led to radical operational changes. This was when I discovered the value of research. As a result our business rapidly diversified into other associated products. Our current business model incorporates several divisions under the one brand: retail, my writing and speaking business, an insurance replacement division and a rapidly growing home cinema business that designs, customises and installs home theatres on the scale of MGM.

I call this 'leveraging off the brand'. I can't take credit for all of this, however, as our two sons Justin and Gavin, and daughter Anissa, are capable managers and are responsible for the daily operations. Not surprisingly, this eventually presented us with our biggest challenge.

I have said previously that we have been reluctant to open more stores and lose control of our high standards. It was never about being bigger. It was always about being the best. It's never been about the size of the corporation. It's about the size of the commitment. Besides, it takes serious capital to finance home entertainment retailing and with its low product margins it is expensive to duplicate. Competition is approaching a level where it's easy to see that the 'good old days' are definitely over. It was going to be tough to support four families on executive salaries with one business.

I had two choices: retire or get another job! There was only ever one option. Besides, a quick glance at my career made it obvious that I was ripe for a revival. There was no way this 'old Bull' was going out to pasture! And we all know the story of the 'young Bull' and the 'old Bull'. Standing back and watching the 'young Bulls' grow and discover their own destinies is a reward only a parent can cherish.

As you might expect, Kayleen and I endured a lot of pain in the early days of our business development. But with the right effort and successfully balancing our business values with family values, we made enormous gains in the stability and happiness of our family unit.

Yes I am wise, but it's wisdom borne of pain. Yes I paid the price, but look how much I gained.

Helen Reddy – 'I am Woman'

Ripe for revival

All my years in retailing have led me to the conclusion that if I were to start another business it would be without *the three nasties*: stock, salaries and rent. By the time overheads and taxation are met, the last person that gets paid is me. That's not really smart. The people who are smart are those who used their own IP (intellectual property) to earn money, much as authors and recording artists do by collecting royalties on income that is paid long after the work is done.

Because our business won many prestigious awards, I was often asked to tell others how we achieved this success. Over time I improved my presentations and enjoyed the experience. Eventually I began to be remunerated for my work and discovered an opportunity to again leverage off the brand and create a new business. This time I was to follow my instincts and use my own (IP) experience to '*be*' the product. I decided to become a professional business presenter. I made the time to write a book about our business experiences, to raise my profile. I got a publishing deal with national distribution and the book became a good seller.

Gradually my fortunes changed, or I should say my direction changed. I had reinvented myself and found a new business opportunity, one that had less competition and zero overheads as it relied on just *my* knowledge. As the speakers bureaus discovered the 'raging Bull' the phones started ringing and so did the cash registers with sales of my book. The royalty cheques began. It was then that I discovered residual income. I had created another source of income in a totally different way from anything I could have ever imagined and yet I was still leveraging off my business. And so, *A Little Bull Enterprises* (my speaking and my books) became another division of our business network. Again Jack Collis's advice, 'work smarter not harder', had stood by me. However, I believe the best is yet to come.

A new opportunity

During my business seminars I don't tell the audience how *they* should do it, I simply tell them how *I* do it, by sharing ideas and concepts that have worked for me. Being a hands-on practitioner with real experience brings obvious credibility to my presentations. Most of my audiences are like-minded souls who relate to the rigours and regulations of business survival and are eager for entrepreneurial inspiration and fresh ideas. The forward thinkers often ask about new business opportunities and the direction in which my experience is taking me. *Enjoying multiple streams of income is my best answer.* Let me share with you the power of residual income streams.

Dead or dead broke

There are no longer 'jobs for life' and the gold watch is now a myth. Companies are merging, downsizing and seeking efficiencies and economies of scale to stay relevant in a global arena that has only one master – the stock market. Publicly listed companies have two sets of customers: their shareholder investors and their traditional core clients. It is difficult to serve two masters. We live in volatile times where nothing is forever and corporate loyalty has been replaced by insidious political agendas for survival or growth. Employment values have changed and the unpredictable needs to be factored into the security of an ageing workforce. People will need to consider their future financial security as, after forty years in the workforce, many may find themselves broke with only five per cent expected to achieve their retirement goal.

> **Fact file**: Eight per cent of people aged fifty-five and over claim to have allocated pensions and annuities and five per cent say they have managed trust funds. (Ray Morgan Research)

Two types of streams – linear and residual

In the future, people will need a portfolio of income streams from different and diversified sources. I don't mean getting a part-time job, but the kind of stream that you can own and control, without marching to the beat of someone else's drum. I mean an independent income that is recurring and continues to flow whether you're there or not. Just as when an inventor gets a payment every time a patent is used and an author or songwriter receives a royalty each time a book or a song is sold or publicly broadcast;

or like successful network marketers, people who leverage the efforts of others by working with a network of associates. These are examples of residual income, income that keeps flowing to you even when you are not working; products that people keep buying long after you've stopped selling them. There are businesses that provide *residual* income with very small start-up costs.

Targeting a new business

When you work for the boss or yourself and get one pay cheque, that's *linear* income. Lose your job and you lose your total income source. In many cases, there is little potential for redemption. In this era of uncertainty, it is wise to have multiple streams of income in your portfolio. The wealthy have always known this and have built wealth by leveraging off the needs and efforts of others. If one income stream dries up they have many more to support them. This is why the gap is widening between the 'haves' and 'have-nots'. If you are to get on the right side of the ledger, you should consider developing a residual stream of income to complement your linear income. Many have done this by diversifying into a property portfolio, although this takes capital or equity.

> **Fact file**: Ninety-five per cent of people have inadequate
> superannuation to fund early retirement if they are forced to take it.

What proportion of your income is residual? If you want to protect against the unknown and provide for a future lifestyle that allows you to do *what* you want *when* you want, then *now* is perhaps the time to consider switching income streams. Let me introduce you to a new direction I have taken. Like all opportunities, it happened when I least expected it!

A health and wealth solution

With the population ageing and as the 'baby boomers' head towards retirement, the two priorities of this huge market segment will be *health* and *wealth*.

These are the industries with strong future growth potential. Let me explain why.

Markets change in commerce, due to a switch in consumer priorities causing market segmentation to evolve. The one segment of the market that has always influenced shifts in consumer trends in the past fifty years has been the 'baby boomer' segment. One of the biggest population explosions the world has seen happened in the eighteen-year period post World War II (1946–1964).

> **Fact file**: Research shows the boomers represent one-third of the world's population.

A need for housing created the property booms and busts of the seventies and eighties. As this society of boomers became affluent, massive waves of consumerism ignited the explosion of the super brands: Disney, Nike, Sony, as well as the super trends: rock 'n' roll, supermarkets, shopping malls, fast food and the internet.

Everything was accessible to those who wanted it and as this mass homogenisation of new lifestyle cultures emerged, the culture vultures wanted everything. Driven by peer pressure and goaded by saturation marketing which promoted too much choice, the boomers were held captive under the hypnotic spell of these new commercial cultures. Not surprisingly, the biggest consumer debt level in history was recorded as a result of the harsh realities of economic globalisation. Easy access to credit, advancement in new technologies and the proliferation of new products and trends radically transformed previous commerce traditions. Nothing could stop this flowing tide of consumerism as it aged and lifestyles changed. Like the glaciers thousands of years ago changed landscapes for ever, nothing could stand in the way of this force.

> **Fact file**: Consumers aged fifty-five and over control thirty-nine per cent of the nation's wealth and are asset rich. (Roy Morgan Research)

Contrary to what the fast-food franchisers would have you believe, their products were simply a result of a consumer switch to a more convenient lifestyle. It is interesting to see a switch away from these traditions as consumer awareness toward a healthier lifestyle manifests itself. The cola bottle by the TV is being replaced by the water bottle at the gym.

Fact file: Fifty per cent of people aged fifty-five and over assert that a low-fat diet is a way of life for them. (Roy Morgan Research 2004)

We work to live, not live to work.

There are three things we all want as a result of the efforts of our working life.

1. *Good* **health** to be able to enjoy the rewards from a lifetime of business and family building.

2. *Better* **wealth** – financial independence from an income stream flowing continually to provide comfort, security and all the things that support a lifestyle to which we have become accustomed.

3. *Best* **lifestyle** – time to spend the best years of your life doing the things that please you.

Coincidence or opportunity?

About a year ago, a participant in one of my business seminars asked for an appointment to discuss a new product and business concept. I always oblige anyone who wants to meet with me, because I strongly believe in people networking. *What you give out always comes back in some way and at some time.* He introduced me to a company that markets nutritional supplements through a network of distributors. As soon as he mentioned network marketing I told him I wasn't interested and just switched off. I couldn't wait to get out of the meeting! I politely accepted some product samples and a video about the company's product development. It sat on my desk for a few days until my son Justin, who manages our electronics division, noticed it. He told me that he had just become a part-time associate of this company to begin earning a residual income. He was surprised at the coincidence of my connection with the same product. However, there is one important lesson I have learned during my long-playing career.

There is no such thing as coincidence – just opportunity!

We are always looking for ways to improve our income stream as it is important to keep cash flowing within the family business. I have always encouraged diversification. When Justin told me it was network marketing, however, I was negative about the concept. After all, I was the marketing guru of the family and my opinion of previous network marketing schemes was less than favourable. I can be a stubborn 'old Bull' when I want to be with an attitude that I'm not always right – but I'm never wrong! I was wrong on this occasion.

Justin said, 'Dad, take these products and you will see why. You need to be taking proper nutritional supplements.' His mind was made up, as he had done extensive research on the company. He was impressed with the quality of the product and the people associated with it, and could identify with the income potential of this business. More importantly, he saw an improvement in his own health, as well as that of his young children.

With my busy lifestyle, travel commitments and energy-sapping business presentations, I am understandably drained when I return home. I discovered that the product boosted my energy levels and noticeably improved my general wellbeing. I was surprised at the unexpected benefits I experienced both physically and mentally and, for he first time in memory, I survived winter without the flu.

Besides, whenever I play my old rock 'n' roll records from the sixties, memories of my youth come flooding back. As we age we like to feel how we did when we were younger. The realisation that I have given rock 'n' roll the best years of my life, and having to accept that *my* best years are behind me, is really scary! I'm sure you baby boomers know what I mean! They say you are only as old as you feel, and I was feeling my best in years.

I became one of Justin's first customers and have been taking the products ever since. It soon became apparent I was in need of proper supplementary nutrition. I was too busy trading hours for dollars and maintaining my businesses without maintaining my body. I began to understand why Justin was interested in becoming an associate, because if the product worked for him, it would work for others. At his insistence I researched the company.

I discovered that this publicly listed company is experiencing explosive growth in the US and is rated as one of the top five companies on the NASDAQ. Its focus is to market a very exclusive range of the finest nutritional products in the world, designed and engineered by one of the world's leading experts in cellular nutrition, a visionary, Dr Myron Wentz. His company is rapidly expanding globally, with its growth a direct result of a superior product and an ageing population of boomers seeking quality health products. The products are not sold through traditional distribution channels where the end price is determined by the 'middle men' in the distribution chain. They are marketed direct to the consumer through a modern people networking system and the company shares its profits with its distributors (associates) through the business of network marketing.

Network marketing – the power of leverage

Network marketing has been around for years but the application of modern incentive techniques to an established business model has proved to be a winner. It works by building a network of associates who assist each other

The independence of your business

to generate residual income, hence the network structure encourages a sense of common purpose and being part of a team, because everyone enjoys the financial benefits of each other's efforts.

This concept of teamwork is at the very core of the network's remuneration plan. Like any business you can only create wealth when you create *leverage*. The difference with this business is that leverage is not bought through large payrolls and high retail rents. All participants can benefit, not just the boss at the top, as in traditional business.

Let me explain what I mean. Imagine after one month you introduce one other person, Jan, into this business. A fairly modest achievement! Then you teach Jan to do the same. So in your second month there is yourself and Jan and you each manage to introduce one new associate. Again you teach the system. In your third month there are four of you (yourself and Jan and your two new associates) and you each introduce just one person. Now there are eight. Duplicate this process again and there will be sixteen and then thirty-two and then sixty-four. Leverage over time, creates exponential growth. By the twelfth month there would be a team of 4096 people.

Now if you and each of your team were paid a small referral royalty every time one of the company's products was purchased by this team, you can understand the power of leverage equates to wealth, not just money, but a recurring income that is no longer dependent on your efforts. And of this huge team of people, you personally introduced just one per month. As your team is growing, some people will join from other states and eventually other countries, which further stabilises your business with an international currency spread, and you haven't even left your home.

This business appeals to me because its principles incorporate all of the things I have been talking about: leveraging, residual income, minimal start-up costs and no overheads. The three nasties are gone!

New growth industries

While network marketing has come of age and is a new growth industry, through research, I could see that 'wellness' was also a growth business of the future.

As a large segment of the population moves toward retirement, many will face a health and wealth dilemma. Health care becomes more important if you want to enjoy the benefits of leisure time, and so does the ability to create residual income to support benefits after retirement. One reason why the *wellness industry* will be one of the next economic booms is that the baby boomers are heading for retirement and want to reclaim their youth. They have the market power to do so and they want wellness and financial security.

Connecting science with wellness

Understanding how to take *good* business basics and make them *better*, until you become the *best* in your market, is the core objective of this book. The quality of the product or service you are selling always determines the long-term success of the business. Success in business requires a unique product that attracts repeat and continuous consumer demand.

Twenty years ago, franchising provided huge opportunities to a section of the workforce that sought independent employment. The successful franchisers were those that marketed a unique product with a duplicative business model. Today the same opportunity exists with home-based businesses with minimal overheads, driven by modern network marketing business development systems. The key is to choose an industry that provides unique products which lead to continuous consumption. Products that support health and wellness are the basis of such an industry.

Top US economist and author of the bestselling book *The Wellness Revolution*, Paul Zane Pilzer, is predicting that the next trillion dollar global industry by the year 2010 will be the wellness industry. He claims: 'Wellness is the taking of products and services when you are not necessarily sick.' He says: 'The consumer has an unlimited propensity to consume wellness products, because no matter how great you feel when you visit a fitness club you want to feel even better.'

Let's take a look at why this is so.

Keeping our bodies healthy so we can perform every day to maximum capacity is a discipline of utmost importance. Yet it is a discipline ignored by many people. Why do we take our health for granted? Why is it we only pay attention to our wellbeing when we get sick or receive a serious wakeup call? Unfortunately in our lifelong objectives of career and family building and our obsessive pursuit of material possessions, we easily drive ourselves to exhausting lengths to maintain performance levels. When sickness inevitably occurs, there is a reactive approach to illness instead of a proactive attitude toward its prevention. The basics of prevention are largely ignored.

Fact file: Ninety-five per cent of health dollars are spent on reactive remedies.

In his book *Invisible Miracles*, Dr Wentz says: 'Health and time are two precious assets that we rarely recognise or appreciate until they have been depleted. As with time, health is the raw material of life. You can use it wisely or waste it or even kill it.' He goes on to say, 'Although it has been said that time is money, in truth, time is much more than money. Money spent or lost can be earned again. Time spent is gone forever and is directly related to the quality of your health.'

This message is profound to me. I had a friend who was a work-a-holic who thought he was invincible. He had an obsessive work ethic because he planned for financial freedom in retirement as a result of his life's work. He had a heart attack at age sixty-six, one year after retirement. What a waste!

Fact file: Sixty to seventy per cent of heart disease could have been prevented with proper diet and exercise.

In the early 1900s the world's leading causes of premature deaths were infectious diseases or conditions that resulted from them: diphtheria, tuberculosis and pneumonia. Today the world's leading causes of premature deaths are degenerative diseases: heart, cancer, stroke and diabetes. These are diseases of affluent societies.

Personal health has to be a priority for every breadwinner.

Fact file: According to world health authorities, 600 million suffer from high blood pressure, 300 million are obese, 194 million suffer from diabetes, 165 million suffer from arthritis, 130 million suffer from asthma.

Prevention is better than cure

Many chronic degenerative diseases can be prevented if the body isn't deprived of the vital nutrients it needs to stay healthy. This deprivation has mainly been brought about by global development causing soil, water and air pollution, radiation from the sun and the depletion of nutrients in the food supply. It is difficult to obtain all the nutrients the body needs from today's foods. This, combined with peer pressures, stress of modern society and poor eating habits, can all contribute to twenty-first century diseases.

The more information I researched on the value of cellular nutrition, the more I began to understand why I was feeling my best in years. A leading international nutritionist warned recently that people eat for palatability, not for nutrition. People eat junk food because it tastes nice, not because it's nutritious. Processed food lacks essential nutrients and more and more doctors are realising the importance of dietary supplements, particularly as the level of pollution is the highest it's ever been. This is a reality of these times. Modern medicine does not have the answers for chronic degenerative disease. The answer is prevention.

You are probably wondering why I am mentioning all this life-threatening stuff in a business book? It's because people are complacent about the most fundamental of issues – good health – and people my age need to take a reality check on how their businesses can continue if the unforeseen happens. You can't take care of your family or your business if you don't have good health. Just as I have devoted considerable attention in this text to the prevention of business ill-health, the consequence of this is that personal health has to be a priority for every breadwinner. I acknowledge that some have personal insurance; however, what good is that to *you* if you're dead! I must admit that my work ethic resembled that of my friend who died at sixty-six!

I have spent the best part of my life managing people and businesses. As successful as this might seem I have neglected to manage my health, which is the most important resource that governs my everyday performance. I believed that a good diet could supply all our nutritional needs, but in this age of atmospheric pollution, I now realise this is not necessarily so.

This has been a big reality check for me. Success in our society is mostly determined by material wealth, but at what cost? The paradox is that we all want the comfortable indulgences that life can provide, but also expect tomorrow to be the same as today. On the one hand we want to create wealth for the future yet on the other we live for the present. What is the true balance of success? How can I consider *my* life successful unless I understand the true definition of success?

Both my parents died prematurely from cancer and heart disease, which may have been prevented. Not a day goes by that I don't think of them and when I look at the veins in my hand I see that they will always be with me. I intend to continue to take nutritional supplements because I regard this as my insurance policy against the degenerative diseases that have plagued our family. The bonus is that the very products that are supporting my health will also support a whole new business opportunity for our family. By taking charge of my own health I am redefining success.

Progress begins when you accept ownership of your own destiny!

BULLET POINTS

- Ambition is the cure for fear.

- We work to live not live to work.

- There is no such thing as coincidence – just opportunity.

- What you give out always comes back in some way and at some time.

- Health and time are two precious assets that we rarely recognise or appreciate until they have been depleted.

THE BULLSEYE PRINCIPLE™

6 DISCIPLINE and DETERMINATION

BE COMMITTED – STAY FOCUSSED

Chapter 19
No is negotiable®

BULLISM™: NEGOTI-A-BULL

> **NO IS NEGOTIABLE®**

Barry Bull

The Bullseye Principle is my secret weapon to target success, and No is Negotiable is the silver bullet I use to hit the Bullseye every time. It is the difference between playing the game and winning the game because persistence always defeats resistance.

We all like to claim a little fame in our life, and if there is one thing I am known for it is my catch cry … *No is Negotiable*. I never take *No* for an answer and by having this attitude I can turn eighty per cent of *Nos* into *Yeses*. I like to get my own way … and by accentuating the positive – I usually do!

You see *ninety per cent of people give up when they are within ten per cent of achieving their goals*. The one word that stops them is *No!* It's amazing how close some people come to achieving their goals when they give up.

> *Many of life's failures are people who did not realise*
> *how close they were to success when they gave up.*
>
> Thomas Edison

I discovered the power of *No is Negotiable* years ago, surprisingly, from my kids!

When my eldest son Justin was about fifteen he came to me and said, 'Dad can I have twenty bucks? My mate's just arrived and we are off to the movies.' My reply was: 'Sure Justin, however, you must mow the lawn before you go. Do your jobs and then you will get your pocket money.' Do you think Justin raced for the Victa? Nope. Instead he raced for his mother!

He said: 'Mum can I have twenty bucks? My mate's just arrived and we are off to the movies.' His mother said, 'Have you asked your father; what does he say?' Justin replied, 'Dad reckons it's OK, except I have to mow the lawn when I get back.'

Two hours later, the lawn is not mowed, we're down twenty dollars and Justin's at the movies. I said to Kayleen, 'Oh jeez – he got us again. That boy is the master negotiator!'

Sound familiar? Of course it does – they're our children and because we love them we have a weakness which they innocently take advantage of. What my kids were doing was negotiating a *No* for their own positive outcome. Like most kids, they wanted to get their own way and for most of the time, they were getting it! They figured out how to negotiate the system to get what they wanted. They saw how easy it was to challenge the word *No*, particularly if they really wanted something. The innocence of youth can simplify the most challenging circumstances. We can all learn from this uncomplicated simplicity.

I wondered if this tactic would work for me in business. I decided to give it a go. And by taking the 'Bull by the horns', surprisingly I began to turn negatives into positives at a surprising rate! Here's how it works.

My secret weapon

Whenever I am confronted with a *No* I challenge it and through negotiation, do my best to turn a negative into a positive. I discovered to my surprise that, more often than not, I would succeed. When I didn't I would reach for my *secret weapon*.

It's a rubber stamp which reads *No is Negotiable*. Whenever I receive a written negative response to a project, I stamp the document with my *secret weapon* and return it! This usually provokes a response that opens up discussion. You cannot begin negotiation without communication. And the Bullfight begins!!

The following story has become a favourite at my business presentations because it tells how I discovered the power of not giving up. It's an example of how persistence overcame resistance, and on this occasion, how 'A little Bull went a long way.'

Born to rock 'n' roll

We have presented many celebrities at Toombul over the past twenty-five years, but the one superstar I really wanted to meet was my long-time favourite rock 'n' roll icon, Cliff Richard. Growing up in the sixties was the most exciting time of my life. I didn't realise it at the time, but my destiny was being shaped by a music revolution called rock 'n' roll, and my early music mentors were Elvis and Cliff.

Over the years, I had sent countless requests to Cliff's record company EMI for him to make an appearance at Toombul and do an album signing while he was on tour, but it never happened. It was 1988 and one week before Cliff was due to appear at his Brisbane concert. I had sent all the letters of request to his record company but to no avail. I just couldn't come up with the right reason for Cliff to come and promote his new album and meet his fans. I needed a different strategy; after all … strategy is knowing what to do next.

'What can I do to get Cliff to come?' I pondered. My answer came in a most unexpected way.

It was Thursday, a late shopping night as I recall, when the Lord Mayor of Brisbane, Sallyanne Atkinson, walked into my store. The elections were getting close and she was on the campaign trail. When I saw Sallyanne, I had an idea. I knew how I could get Cliff. I said: 'Sallyanne, what are you doing next Thursday?'

She gave me a curious look and asked, 'Why, Barry?'

I said, 'I'm planning to present Cliff Richard next week out on the centre stage where he'll be signing his new album and meeting his fans. It just occurred to me when you walked in, that it would be *so* appropriate if you could be here to welcome Cliff to Brisbane. There will be thousands of people here and lots of media, and this wouldn't do your re-election campaign any harm either.' I duly informed her to a chorus of a thousand invisible violins how much Cliff's music meant to so many Queenslanders, and how special it would be if the Lord Mayor of Brisbane could welcome this outstanding celebrity. 'What a touch of class it would add, Sallyanne, and perhaps you could make a presentation of some kind to him.' I think at this point I got out the 'air guitar' and started to sing, *We're all going on a summer holiday.* I was on a real roll.

At that moment her eyes lit up and I knew she was a fan. I could see the thought of meeting Cliff had real appeal. So she turned to her secretary and asked: 'What am I doing next Thursday?'

The secretary looked in her diary and replied: 'You are at Westfield, Indooroopilly.'

I could see another *No* coming up, so before she could say anything I said: 'My dear Lord Mayor, there will be nobody at Indooroopilly next Thursday, they will all be *here* to see Cliff.'

She thought for a moment then said to her secretary. 'Cancel Indooroopilly.' With an election-winning smile she turned to me and announced, 'I'll be here. Ring the office tomorrow to make the arrangements.' With that, she walked out.

I thought to myself … '*Wow, unbelievable,* I've got the Lord Mayor of Brisbane to present Cliff Richard … I just have one problem … I don't have Cliff Richard to present to the Lord Mayor!'

The next day I phoned Cliff's manager to tell him the news. At this point I want to fast forward this story three years, because of course he came. In fact Sir Cliff has done five exclusive promotions with us at Toombul in the past fifteen years.

It was 1991 … three years later. We had just completed a hugely successful promotion with him at the store that day and he invited me to dinner after the concert that evening. During dinner he said to me, 'Barry, I was in the room when you called that day and my manager put his hand over the phone and said to me, "I've got this guy Barry Bull from Toombul Music on the phone ... he's got the Lord Mayor of Brisbane to welcome you and she is going to present you with a citizenship scroll to the city. He expects three thousand people to turn up as well as the media."' Then he said: 'We poms have a way of saying "yes"!' And he just looked at me and gave me the thumbs up. I've had the finger many times in my life, folks, so that thumb looked real good.

I thought to myself, 'Was that all it took?' Over the years he knew who I was and what I wanted. I was always ninety per cent of the way ... the word stopping me from achieving my goal had been *No*! By not taking *No* for an answer, I had just crossed the line. This was the birth of my biggest business hit, *No is Negotiable*!

Back to 1988, and the big day. (We are almost there, so stick with me because I hit a huge Bullseye that day.) A tour bus arrived in the shopping centre car park from Toowoomba, another one came in from Rockhampton, and another from the Gold Coast. They were all packed with Cliff fans. They had hired tour buses as groups to travel to our promotion to see their hero. As they were getting off the buses, some of them wore badges with the words, 'We're on a summer holiday with Cliff', and they had pommy accents. Would you believe that some international fans had taken their holidays in the UK and were following Cliff around the world, going to every concert and seeing him at every opportunity.

Believe me, it's true. *No Bull*! Some fans cannot get enough. I was stunned as I thought to myself, 'I wish I could understand female fantasies.' But Cliff sure does!

That day several thousand people turned out to see Cliff. The shopping centre bulged with business and they all became *our* customers as they queued to have their CD personally autographed.

I have a photograph on my wall of Lord Mayor Sallyanne Atkinson present-ing Cliff with the citizenship scroll to the city. Whenever things get tough and the negatives outnumber the positives, I look at this photograph. It's a powerful reminder to never give up. To never take *No* for an answer.

The story I have told you changed my life, and yet without persistence it wouldn't have happened. It made me realise that if you believe in yourself then anything is possible. All it takes is persistence.

Persistence always defeats resistance

And speaking of persistence ...

Just six months after we presented Cliff, US country superstar John Denver, while on an Oz tour, accepted our invitation to come to the centre and promote his latest musical offering. And, once again, so did the lord mayor. As you can tell I was on a roll with lord mayors and superstars.

The day before John arrived, however, I received a call from the lord mayor's office advising that her schedule had blown out and it was unlikely that she would be on time for our presentation. Sallyanne had an important function to host on the other side of town and because of travel distance she would be late arriving at our event.

Because John's appearance had been heavily advertised, our schedule couldn't be changed. To make matters worse, we had informed Denver's management (and the media) that Lord Mayor Atkinson would welcome John to Brisbane. I had a problem. This time the tables were reversed. I didn't have a lord mayor to present to our celebrity! I had less than twenty-four hours to come up with a solution.

I can't take credit for the helicopter suggestion, but we solved the problem by flying the lord mayor from her morning engagement to arrive in the centre car park, just in time to present John to his adoring fans. It's amazing what a couple of concert tickets and the chance to meet a celebrity can do to a deserving helicopter pilot!

The boy is back in town

While these stories are of memorable events that happened many years ago, like all good stories ... there are more! In 2003, the Bachelor Boy was back in town.

While on his Australian tour, Sir Cliff Richard accepted my invitation to come to Toombul again … for the *fifth* time! He told me that the Toombul appearances has become a tradition … and is the only one he consistently does … anywhere !

My persistence in achieving a dream eventually led to huge business opportunities with all of Cliff's fans. Today our store is *the* retail contact point for hundreds of Cliff's Aussie fans, many of whom are regular customers. Through our data base, and his fan club, we connect with them every time Cliff releases new product. Photos of Cliff and his appearances are on our web site and are downloaded across the world and we regularly export specially signed product to loyal international fans. Who says that one store in the suburbs of Brisbane can't sell to the world!

The message in this story is not to lose focus on your hopes and dreams, as most people never realise how close they are to success when they give up. Cliff's amazing success is also testimony to this. He is an astute businessman who never gives up on a project in which he believes. He consistently reinvents his career, which thrills his fans and baffles his critics.

The millennium prayer

It happened big time at the end of the decade. Cliff recorded the biggest selling song in the UK for that year and he didn't even have a recording contract! The song was 'The Millennium Prayer', an unusual version of the Lord's prayer sung to the tune of 'Auld Lang Syne'. Cliff's long-time UK record company, EMI, decided not to release the song and radio banned its airplay. The lack of support Cliff received from his record company and the media must have been a huge disappointment to him. Despite the negative reaction to the song, however, Cliff proved them wrong and it went on to become one of his biggest hit singles of all time. It is interesting to tell you what happened here.

EMI Australia did not have the rights to the song because of its parent company's decision not to release it. In order to satisfy local fans we imported a thousand singles prior to Christmas and I persuaded a local radio announcer friend to play the song on Brisbane radio 4BH.The phones went berserk, as we were the only store in Brisbane (and probably Australia) to have the song. I recall it went to number one in Brisbane. When the local record industry finally woke up to the phenomenon, EMI rang me for a copy of the single. I promptly told them to bugger off! The song was eventually released by Festival Records, after we satisfied the local fans' inexhaustible demand for this Christmas offering. *The Millenium Prayer* sold 1.4 million copies in the UK.

Something's goin' on

In late 2004, Cliff released a new album that was a total departure from anything he had done before. It was called *Something's Goin' On* and was recorded in Nashville in the US. I knew something was going on from the moment the fans got a whiff of the project and our 'Cliff phone' started ringing. I sensed this was a significant album for him and I wanted to do something special for his fans.

I emailed Cliff's management requesting a phone interview that I could use on my 4BC radio segment. I planned to review the album with him, knowing that this was his first studio album in three years and there would be lots to discuss. I was also preparing an after-hours cocktail party at our store for the week of the album release, exclusive to the Cliff fans that belonged to our VIP Club. Here is the value of a comprehensive customer capture program, as hundreds of Aussie Cliff fans belong to our VIP Club. I not only wanted to surprise them by playing this exclusive interview, but knew they were hanging out for his new CD.

Cliff's management informed me that the interview would be difficult because he was out of the country. I was told that when he returned, he was committed to a busy promotion schedule to work the album in the UK and Europe for Christmas. My chances looked slim.

However, I persisted. *No is Negotiable* – right? Besides, Cliff has always supported my promotion agendas and he knows how important his music is to his loyal Aussie fans. He also had a new album to promote. I was right! One week later Cliff agreed to do my interview.

But it was not that simple. The interview was to be pre-recorded at eight in the morning in the 4BC studio and Cliff was to call me. As I sat waiting for his call, nothing happened. Eventually I received an email indicating the interview had been called off because Cliff could not get through. I sat at the station disappointed, realising that I had missed my opportunity. However, another opportunity was about to unfold!

Unbeknown to me, Queensland Premier Peter Beattie was in the next studio being interviewed on the 4BC breakfast show. We bumped into each other in the corridor. Getting to talk to the premier is as difficult as talking to Cliff Richard. I wasn't about to miss my chance.

Peter had launched my first book in 2001 and with his presence and support over 600 people had attended the occasion. I told him excitedly that I was writing another. Without missing a beat I asked him if he would provide a foreword for my new book and consider launching it in Australia. 'Sure mate,' the premier grinned. 'Just call my office with the details.' Wow – that was easy, I thought, as the premier shook my hand and bolted for the door. I had just scored another Bullseye! And I wasn't about to give up on Sir Cliff either!

That day, I emailed the UK requesting that we try again the next day. I reconfirmed the telephone number Cliff should call so there would be no problem this time. The UK is ten hours behind our time zone, which makes immediate communication difficult. For this reason I didn't get a reply.

The next morning I arrived at the shop to find an urgent email advising that Cliff would call me at eleven in the evening UK time. That made it nine in the morning Brisbane time *today* and I had just fifteen minutes to get to the studio! I really had to 'Move it' and drove like a bat out of hell for the station. Just as I ran into 4BC an excited receptionist yelled, 'Cliff Richard is on the line from the UK for you!' The whole studio just turned and gawked at me when the studio monitor screeched – 'Cliff Richard on line one for Barry!' I just love my job some days!

Cliff gave a remarkable interview. He was so excited about the Nashville sessions that we chatted for twenty minutes about his latest musical milestone. He told me all the songs were specially written for him and rather than overdub the recording, which is a common studio technique, most of the songs were recorded live with a studio packed with polished professional musicians. He said this was the first time he had done this since recording with The Shadows back in the early sixties. 'The *feel* in the studio was amazing, Barry!' he exclaimed. 'Just standing at the mike, watching the live band and hearing these amazing sounds unfold. This session took me in a direction that I hadn't been to before. It was like an adventure for me, musically!' I sensed his excitement and was privileged to share his experience.

After the Nashville sessions, Cliff went to Miami where he recorded a song with Barry Gibb. The tune had Bee Gees stamped all over it. It is a lush ballad that Barry had specially written for him. If you're a music fan then this trivia is for you. If you're not, then ignore this and just read on.

The following Monday night I reviewed Cliff's album on radio with host Tony Murphy, and played the interview the next evening to sixty adoring Cliff fans at our Toombul party. Were they surprised! The look on their faces when they heard him talking to me was indescribable. This is what I mean about rewarding our customers with a unique experience. It is why they are so loyal to us.

And *No is Negotiable* worked *again*! Also I hope you have detected how I achieved (by bumping into the premier) two objectives with the one initiative.

I am not just a fan of Sir Cliff's art; I have strong admiration for his loyalty and integrity. Integrity is so important if we are to have love, trust and loyalty in our lives. Cliff Richard understands this and through his musical legacy continues to reinforce its virtues.

I have learned much from Cliff over the years. He is one of pop music's strongest assets and is a mentor to me. Every few years he gets the urge to raise the quality threshold, reach out to the uncommitted and thereby reinvent his career. By never giving up on his beliefs he has sustained a career for over forty years, and has had more chart success in the UK than Elvis and The Beatles!

Cliff Richard has had 119 single hits, fifty-two international number ones and fifty-nine best-selling albums in his forty-eight-year career. His total global unit sales are approaching 300 000 000. Interestingly his new album is released through Decca Records in the UK, who had turned him down way back in 1958, prompting a forty-year relationship with EMI. Decca also turned down The Beatles in 1963. Apparently they weren't ready to rock 'n' roll!

Cliff Richard is one of the most remarkable entertainers and businessmen I have met. He continually returns my loyalty and I am honoured that he regards me as a friend.

'Barry's imaginative initiatives, support and professionalism have undoubtedly helped shift significant quantities of my product, and that of other artists too. It's become almost a tradition for me to visit Toombul Music during an Aussie tour – simply because the fans are made welcome, it's a fun occasion, and it makes good commercial sense! What I need is a Barry Bull in every town and every country I visit. If only!'

Cliff Richard
April 2005

None of this would have happened if I had accepted *No* for an answer. By persistence and using my secret weapon, *No is Negotiable,* I always have a fair chance of achieving my goals. Think about it – who do you know? A lord mayor, a premier or a celebrity? How can you draw attention to your business? Can you do promotions like this? Can you run events that get the town talking?

Of course you can. Simply remove the negatives between you and your objective. *No is Negotiable,* don't take *No* for an answer, and don't allow others to compromise your dreams. If you accept *No* for an answer the chances are you are accepting a response that supports someone else's mediocrity. Adopt a 'nothing can stop me from succeeding' attitude and do what it takes to achieve your goal. Murphy's law, however, has an ugly habit of

Think about it – who do you know?
A lord mayor, a premier or a celebrity – the Queen?

interfering with your plans along the way. This is the point when most people give up. Just remember when the going gets tough that you are at the ninety per cent mark and life is testing you. Go the extra mile and you will reach your goal. Most worthwhile endeavours are only accomplished by persistence, determination and that little bit extra.

The power of persistence and that little bit extra

While I have related my Cliff Richard story many times, it is a story that remains memorable and never dates because of its powerful message. However, I am often challenged to defend its power.

Not so long ago I spoke at a retail business breakfast in Melbourne. One week later I received an email that contained my *No is Negotiable* logo and a plea for help. Greg Nugent is the owner of Shoppingtown Newsagency at Westfield Doncaster and had attended my session. Greg is a Ticketek agent and had sold two tickets to the John Farnham–Tom Jones concert to a regular customer. The tickets were a gift to her mum. Inadvertently the customer had purchased the ticket for the wrong night and had missed the concert. Her mum was extremely disappointed and appealed to Greg for assistance. There was still one concert to go and there were no guarantees of redemption from Ticketek, so the newsagent took the initiative to contact me.

Greg recalled that I knew John Farnham and reminding me that *No is Negotiable* he appealed to me for help. He clearly wasn't going to take *No* for an answer. I told him I would see what I could do. I called Glenn Wheatley (John's long-time manager) who is an old mate, and fortunately Glenn answered my call. Although busily preparing to video John's forthcoming concert he cheerfully advised me about the procedure to take to solve the problem. You see the reason I called Glenn Wheatley is because the newsagent's customer was *also* Glenn's customer. I passed Glenn's advice on to the newsagent. The next morning Greg Nugent sent me this email message. 'My customer had a wonderful time at the concert. Thank you for all your help in keeping my customers happy!'

It's amazing the results you get when you remove the letter 't' from can't.

An irreplace-a-bull experience

Our celebrity presentations are all examples of discipline and determination. By applying a disciplined approach to our negotiation strategy and never lacking the determination to succeed, we uncovered a way to hit the Bullseye with uncanny accuracy. And this exposed a retailing gem that became a jewel in our crown. We gave more to our customers than just service .We gave them an irreplace-a-bull experience. This winning retail recipe became our point of difference.

> *In order to be irreplaceable one must always be different.*
>
> Coco Chanel

Customer service today is doing what every consumer expects to get but rarely remembers. The closest some merchants get to it, is bidding their clients: "Have a nice day." More often than not, customer service simply hasn't delivered on its promise to make us feel good about how and where we spend our hard earned dollars. The key word here is experience. This is the difference between businesses that promote price and those that provide a consumer experience.

Have you considered lately where your business fits this analogy? What is the experience from the moment your client comes in contact with your business to the moment they leave? Have you looked at the entire experience from marketing, demonstration, fulfilment to usability? Are you easy to do business with? What's your main attraction, your point of difference? Do you know what your customers want, when they want it, and can deliver on that promise every time?

I have strongly targeted customer relationships in this text because it takes discipline and determination to successfully win business today. If you want your best clients to come back then give them a satisfying experience from the beginning to the end. It's what you do after you do what you're expected to do that matters most.

And when those nasty negatives begin to infect performance, use my *No is Negotiable* stamp. Nothing combats a negative disease more effectively!

BULLET POINTS

- Persistence always defeats resistance.

- Don't give up when you still have something to give.

- Ninety per cent of people give up when they are within ten per cent of achieving their goals.

- Don't accept an answer that supports someone else's mediocrity.

- Remove the letter 't' from can't.

- It's what you do after you do what you're expected to do that matters most.

THE
BULLSEYE PRINCIPLE™

7

HIT THE BULLSEYE

REAP THE REWARDS

Chapter 20

Pursue the passion

BULLISM™: LOVE-A-BULL

All you need is love.

Lennon and McCartney

'All You Need is Love', the great Beatles' anthem, was purposely written for the world's first live Telstar satellite broadcast. What a powerful message of peace The Beatles gave to the world. It was sad that no one was listening.

In 1967, the power of technology to send a single global message was already awesome. Three decades later 11 September sent a very different message to the world, a gruesome message, and the world has not been the same since. Journalists spread the message of doom and gloom constantly and the public forum this gives to evil serves only to support their cause. If the horrors of the world weren't publicised there would be nothing to feed them.

In 2004 I travelled overseas for a month and purposely tuned the media off my holiday dial. When I returned the media's preoccupation with the problems in the world was there to greet me – I had missed nothing. I get depressed after the evening news bulletins and yet it is the time of day when the whole family is together. It should be a time for love and high spirits. If love and stories of goodwill were given equal media exposure to sensationalism, then a balance of hope and feel-good emotions would prevail at family time. Positive productivity would result. Instead every television and newspaper headline shouts the dangers of living in a world of global unrest and insecurity. It is difficult to challenge concerns, apprehension and fear when in reality we are fortunate to live in a world that provides more security and more opportunity for prosperity than ever before.

Modern society is burdened by time-poor lifestyles that are underpinned by pressures of all kinds. Why is it that families and close friends who really matter seem to meet only at weddings and funerals? I have had my share of funerals lately and always feel guilty when I see relatives that I should keep in touch with but for reasons I regret I haven't done so – life just gets in the way. John Lennon nailed it when he wrote, 'Life is what happens when we're busy making other plans.'

Have you ever stopped to think that the most special occasions in our lives are always those occasions when we are with our loved ones? I have also had my share of weddings lately.

I honestly love you

In the autumn of 2004, our daughter Anissa was married. One of the most special occasions in a father's life is to walk his only daughter down the aisle on her wedding day. It was a joyous occasion and being a little bloke I rarely get to feel ten feet tall. I was so proud as I saw the special beauty in my little girl as only a parent can. Her radiance captivated all who shared her special day.

As father of the bride I was duty bound to make a speech and, always the spokesman, there were high expectations of me to make an entertaining testimonial to the newlyweds. Instead, when my turn came, I gave her 'words and music' which was unexpected. With the accompaniment of my guitar, I sang my daughter a song that contained a special lyric, a dedication of my love for her, to the melody of Olivia's big hit 'I Honestly Love You', with a simultaneous slide presentation of her twenty-six years. It was a very melancholy moment for everyone.

You might ask what this has to do with business? Well, love is the most important ingredient in the business of life and the most successful people I know are those who are happy and who have successfully balanced family values with business values. They love what they do. They are the wealthiest people of all and it has got nothing to do with money.

> *Success is not the key to happiness. Happiness is the key to success.*
>
> Herman Caine

Loving what you do

At the tender age of fifteen I discovered Elvis and have loved rock 'n' roll music ever since. I have had the good fortune to select a career all those years ago in an industry that brings so much happiness to so many people. I have also been fortunate to have the opportunity to meet and work with some of the biggest entertainers on the planet. When I watch them work they all have one thing in common: their love of performing. The most successful entertainers I have met are those who are passionate about their profession and love what they do. Because of this, they do it consistently well.

They began by being *good*, rehearsed and performed until they got *better* and because of their passion they became the *best*. Sound familiar? It is these entertainers who are *my* business mentors and who helped shape my *Bullseye Principle*.

Have you ever wondered why entertainment icons like Slim Dusty, John Farnham, Cliff Richard, Neil Diamond, Rod Stewart and Tom Jones have sustained careers for three and four decades? It's because they love what they do. Brilliant entertainment careers have been built around a passion that creates a huge and loyal supportive fan (customer) base. They know what music to record because they know what their fans want. They then take this product to their market with well-timed concert tours.

I am often asked if I have a favourite entertainer who stands out above all the rest. There is one ... and the following story is a highlight at my speaking engagements. It is a story of one man's lifelong pursuit of his passion ... and I *love* to tell it.

The most successful people I know are those who are happy.

Looking Forward, Looking Back, was Slim Dusty's one hundredth album. For any artist to record one hundred albums is very rare; however, our Slim did just that.

(Slim Dusty recorded 107 albums in his fifty-plus year career and sold eight million units of all formats for label EMI.)

Several years ago, Channel Nine presented Slim on 'This Is Your Life', paying tribute to the man and his career. A million Aussies watched it, including me, and some of you I suspect. An idea formed in my mind. I wanted Slim to come to Toombul to promote his latest offering. I knew he was going to be headlining at the Gympie Muster (an annual country music festival about 150 km north of Brisbane) in a few weeks' time. So I called his record company and asked the question. 'Absolutely not!' was the response. 'Slim is seventy-four years old and doesn't do shopping centre promotions any more!'

'*Bulldust*!' was my reply. 'You haven't even asked him.' But the answer was still *No*! You know by now how I hate taking *No* for an answer from record companies. It's like *a red rag to a Bull!*

I had an idea. There's no monopoly on good ideas, particularly if the idea is mine in the first place. I wondered if the tactic I had used to bring Cliff Richard to Toombul all those years before would work again. I decided to give it a go.

I discovered that Queensland Premier Peter Beattie was a big Slim fan, and the premier doesn't live too far from our shop. Through a mutual friend, I sent a personally autographed copy of Slim's new album to his home with a note saying that as he is a fan of Slim's music I hoped he would enjoy his new album. I then sent a letter of request to the premier's department, requesting that the premier present Slim with a recognition award for his hundredth album recording achievement.

Usually you would expect some time to pass before you received a reply to such an unusual request, but not on this occasion! The very next day the premier's department called me and said, 'The premier has accepted your invitation – he is a big Slim Dusty fan and he would love to meet him.'

I said, '*Really*! I'd never have guessed!'

I then called Slim's manager and told him that the premier wanted to present Slim with an award and could Slim come to Toombul, accept the award, sign his new album and meet the fans. His manager replied, 'I don't think that will be a problem, Barry, we are going to be up your way soon at the Gympie Muster.'

I said, grinning to myself, I didn't think that would be a problem either!

It was a Saturday when I was to present Slim. As it turned out, I was faced with three problems! The first was that his manager told me Slim would not perform, he would not sing, he would be there only to meet the fans, accept the award, and sign his new album. The second problem was that Slim had to perform at 'the muster' that night so I had to present him at twelve noon. The third problem was Premier Peter Beattie was in Weipa in far north Queensland that day and was not due back in Brisbane until one o'clock. I had one hour to fill in.

At midday I welcomed Slim to a thousand adoring fans. They went crazy when they saw him. I said, 'Slim all of these folk are your loyal fans and they all have a Slim Dusty story. However, would you mind if I told you *mine*?'

'Sure mate,' he said, with a curious look in his eyes, which beamed under that famous bush hat. As I began, a hush fell over the huge crowd.

'Slim, I began my career in a music store in Brisbane in 1958. During my first week, my job was to go to the record companies to pick up the records that were selling well, to restock the store. Slim, I'm a little fellow now and I was a little fellow then and seventy-eight records were the standard in those days. They were real heavy to carry.'

'I remember them,' Slim replied. 'My early recordings were on seventy-eights.'

'Well, Slim, one week into my job I slipped and fell in the street and smashed fifty of the buggers!' I shouted.

'My golly,' Slim said. 'What happened?'

'My boss called me into his office and I knew I was in big trouble,' I replied. 'My boss said, "Barry you have only been in the job a week and you have already cost the company money. You have just smashed fifty records! I don't think you're suited to retailing. Can you give me a reason why I shouldn't dismiss you?"

'Slim I was so close to getting fired and the only excuse I could think of was ... "Sir, can I help it if Slim Dusty sells more records than I can carry!" Because, that was *your* record mate ... it was "A Pub with No Beer"!'

Slim grinned and shouted, 'That was the record I had on seventy-eight!'

'Well, your sales went backwards by fifty that week, mate,' I replied!

'Did you keep your job?' he asked.

'Yep!' I grinned. 'My boss said "Barry Bull, you are only fifteen and five foot nothing. I will give you another chance." He accepted my lame excuse, and it was then Slim I realised ... *A Little Bull Goes a Long Way!*'

Slim grinned at me and said, 'That could be a good title for a book!'

I got real serious and said, 'Slim, as *that* song has been *your* career record, and as *that* song almost cost me *my* career ... what do you reckon we sing the first verse together?' The crowd roared their approval at this unexpected entertainment. Slim grinned at me, knowing I was well outside the square.

His manager was not grinning. He was yelling at me from backstage, 'Kill the bugger ... kill the bugger!' The entertainer kicked in, however, and Slim turned to me and said, 'Sure mate, why not.' And he put his arm around my shoulder and together, unaccompanied, we sang the first verse of 'A Pub with No Beer'.

As we finished, the crowd went bananas and yelled for more! Slim turned to me with a smile all over his face, loving every minute of the occasion. He said ... 'Let's do the second verse!'

I said, 'I don't know the second verse!'

He replied, 'I do, can I do it?'

I said, 'It's your song, mate, you can do what you like!'

So off he went and sang the second verse of 'The Pub ...' and it was like a genie had popped out of the bottle! A magic spell was cast over the huge crowd. What I mean by this is, if you mix an emotional experience with a great retail offer, the result is customer mania!

Everybody bolted for our store and bought every Slim Dusty record they could lay their hands on. For the next hour they queued up and Slim signed their albums, had his photo taken and happiness beamed from everyone's face. It was clear to me that Slim loved every minute of the occasion as well.

An hour later Premier Beattie arrived and presented Slim with an award that was so big I could hardly see over the top! As our premier never goes anywhere without channels Nine and Seven strapped to his back, the event made the six o'clock news!

Looking Forward Looking Back became one of Slim's most successful albums and peaked at number three on the national charts. It is my favorite Slim album for several reasons. He came to Toombul to assist me to promote this album and it was the last time we would work together. Also it contains some fine songs and the Don Walker composition title track was written *for* Slim as the closing lyric testified.

Making songs from what I know ... looking forward, looking back.

Unfortunately, there is a sad end to this story, as Slim Dusty passed away on 19 September 2003. Australia lost a national treasure and those who knew him lost a great mate. Over the years, I became friends with Slim (he gave me a wonderful testimonial for my book cover and thanks to him I called it *A Little Bull Goes a Long Way*) and I came to realise how much he loved his work. He told me once he would perform until the day he died, because he understood how much his music meant to his fans. He did just that. His last album, *Columbia Lane*, contained just seven songs he had recorded until ill health took its toll. Every Slim fan has a Slim Dusty story. He had that kind of impact on everyone he met. He just made you feel that he was *your* mate.

This is *my* story, and I know Slim would have loved the thought of me telling it, as he liked to make people happy. I loved the man and his music, and so do many Aussies. His love of country music took him to the bright lights of the cities, and some of the most remote corners of Australia.

Love is all you need!

Tommy at Toombul

Tommy Emmanuel is another great Australian whose music I enjoy and good friendship I value.

The title of Tommy's latest album, *Endless Road*, couldn't be more apt – after all, this extraordinary guitarist and entertainer has clocked up more kilometres than he could possibly count in his quest to take his music to the world. Tommy's talents have long been recognised in his native Australia, and he's now winning accolades throughout the United States and Europe for his evocative, powerful, expressive guitar music and his skills as a spellbinding performer.

It was late August, 2004, that my friend was back in Oz where he was engaged to perform at the Gympie Muster. On his way, Tommy stopped off at the centre to do a special performance for us to promote his new album. As he has lived in the US for several years, I hadn't seen him since last time he came to Toombul, four years previously.

He arrived at the centre earlier than expected because he needed some assistance in repairing the electronics on one of his Maton guitars. He knew I would help out. After an emotional reunion I took him to our upstairs offices where we set about disembowelling his famous Maton. In our boardroom he noticed my 'wall of fame', which contains photographs of all the artists who have performed for us at Toombul over the past 20 years. This fascinated Tommy as he saw himself in the company of dozens of other celebrities. His eyes fixed on the photo of Slim Dusty and me.

Tommy was also a great mate of Slim. I related the story behind the photo of Slim and me singing 'The Pub with No Beer', and told him that Slim had been recording up until his untimely death. We both agreed he was an inspiration to all Aussies.

Tommy turned to me and said, 'Baz, I want to tell you another story that inspired me and also inspired Slim.'

'It's a story of an American country music legend, the late Jimmie Rodgers, whose dedication to music was much like Slim's. Not a lot of people would know who he is but to many he is the father of country music. His career started in the early nineteen twenties until his death in 1933. What inspired me about him was he knew he was dying of tuberculosis and his music was so important to him that he spent his last days recording. He lived in the south and travelled by paddle steamer up the Mississippi, took a train to the east coast, and then another to New York City, where he checked himself into a hotel. He then went into a recording studio, had a bed brought in and would record one song at a time. Then he would rest. When he finally finished recording he went back to the hotel, where he died.'

Tommy gave me a most intense look as he said: 'Here was a man who spent his last energy recording so he could get his music to the world. That to me was a great inspiration and his music inspired many great country artists that followed.'

I have said before that my mentors include the wonderful musicians and artists who give so much through their music and professional ability. I have always sourced inspiration from their artistry and attitude toward pleasing their audiences. I have found a great similarity in attitude, in pleasing our customers. It fascinates me to listen to *my* mentors describe *their* mentors.

And that was only the beginning.

One hour later I introduced Tommy on the centre stage to an enthusiastic audience who had been waiting patiently for his performance. As tradition has it, I always interview my guests to provide a personal connection about their music to their fans. I fully understand that if I do my job and the artist does theirs, then all these fans become very satisfied customers.

One of the songs on his new album was a tribute to the great Chet Atkins, Tommy's lifelong mentor. Chet, who was the master of finger picking guitar technique, died in 2001. I asked Tommy how his friend's passing had affected *his* life.

'I still feel his presence you know!' Tommy replied. 'In fact, on this album, there's a song called "Chet's Ramble". He began to describe how he composed his tribute to this legendary musician.

'It was 30 June 2002, which was the anniversary of his passing. I got up early in the morning at my home in England, went down to my office and put on a CD of his music. I thought, how can I celebrate his life? I found a box of tapes that we were working on when we were writing songs for the album we did together, *The Day Finger Pickers Took Over the World*. There were some songs we didn't finish, so I thought rather than mourn his passing what better way to honour his life than to write a song for him. I found this little melody, so I wrote a second part to it and by using all the musical tools I had learned from him, it turned out the way I knew he would have played it.'

As we discussed the album content the similarity with my business attitudes and his became apparent.

Tommy had recorded two beautiful renditions of the chestnuts, 'Over the Rainbow' and 'Mona Lisa'. I asked him his reason for including two classic evergreens on an album of mainly self-compositions. He said that these were two songs that he'd been playing at his shows for a long time and so many people had asked him to record them. 'I always listen to the people who support me. You need to listen to the people that you are playing to, so you can find out what they want,' he said. Makes sense to me.

> *Listening to your customers and giving them what they want*
> *is a fundamental of customer retention.*

He said, 'Whenever I'm teaching young people, I always ask them the question: What is it that you're trying to achieve when you go out on stage to play? What is your goal?' They usually say, 'To have a good time and entertain the people.' I tell them, 'What you want to hear is … everybody coming up to you at the end of the night and asking … *when are you coming back*? That's what you're aiming for, because in life we all need something good to do, we all need a gig. So you've got to get out there and give it you're best effort every time, if you want to become the best.'

There were budding guitar players in the audience aged from seven to seventy, and they hung on his every word. He was their hero and Tommy, sensing the opportunity, took a moment to inspire them. His words also had a profound effect on me because what he was talking about was my *good, better, best* belief … *The Bullseye Principle.*

He had inspired me with the Jimmy Rodgers story, now he was inspiring young players in his presence. I was again learning from a master motivator and he hadn't even played a note.

He then took the stage and did the notes flow. For the next thirty minutes he enthralled his audience with his amazing artistry. Our customers loved it. So did Tommy as he settled in to meet the fans and autograph his product.

I first met Tommy Emmanuel way back in the seventies when he was playing with his brother Phil at the Sunnybank Hotel in Brisbane. He was a *good* guitarist. Each time he came to Toombul for me over the years, he was *better* than before. Today Tommy is one of the world's *best*. But don't take my word for it. Before his passing, Chet Atkins' said, 'Tommy Emmanuel is the best finger picker in the world!'

It was a pleasurable day for us both, and as we parted, neither of us could say much, as true friends bid farewell. I gave him a few CDs to listen to, of some great Aussie guitar players. I know the music he likes and he knew it was my way of saying thanks.

When words fail, music speaks
Anon.

BULLET POINTS

- Life is what happens when we're busy making other plans.

- Success is not the key to happiness. Happiness is the key to success.

- Pursue the passion.

Chapter 21

A road map for business success

BULLISM™: DO-A-BULL

The best way to predict your future is to create it.

Anon.

The *Bullseye Principle* has benefited me greatly in my life. It is my personal strategy: to create an objective, stretch limits and measure performance while maintaining the discipline to stay focussed on what it is I'm trying to achieve. It's a simple road map of business-building principles that puts priorities in place and signposts the way forward. Without a business plan to follow it's easy to lose your way, particularly when dealing with the endless distractions that are part of everyday life. We all have dreams and ambitions but because of the demanding consequences of balancing business values with family values, it is quite easy to become addicted to distractions.

It took me many years to analyse what I had learned from adversity and had gained from the time when life was less complex than it is today. I discovered that all my dreams and ambitions became reality when I targeted them. Once I focussed on a target (such as winning a national Westfield award), I was rewarded and recognised. This encouraged me to keep dreaming. Everyone needs a dream.

If you don't have a dream, how are you going to make one come true?

Anon.

A road map for business success

The reason most people don't achieve their goals is they never really set them in the first place. We all need to turn our dreams into goals and set a target for achieving them, not just in business but as a fundamental necessity of our life. Because we live in a drive-through world, we can easily get caught up in irrelevant matters and lose track of basic values. We often need a prescription to help us get back on track.

The adoption of this goal-setting principle is a prescription to help you to stay focussed on what it is you want to achieve and to establish a target for how you are going to get it. Even if it means stretching the limits a little.

Stretching limits

I see Australians from all walks of life with the desire to achieve every day. In their own way, they each have their own targeted goals. We all have a favourite weekend recreational place that we visit as frequently as possible, a magnet that attracts our thoughts and desires with positive energy and makes us feel at ease.

Mooloolaba on Queensland's beautiful Sunshine Coast is mine. The tranquility of the area, and the exhilaration of an early morning walk, do something special to the soul. It provides me with a much needed sense of spirituality and seems to miraculously heal the wounds from the business battlefield from which I have just retired. The sand between my toes is an exhilarating counterbalance to the tension between my ears.

I enjoy the walk along the beach early in the morning and out along the breakwater that shelters the mouth of the Mooloolah River. At the end of the breakwater is a light beacon that marks the northern approach to the river. It's a landmark of sorts, but to me it's a beacon for peace. This is where you will find me on most Sunday mornings when the weather is at its best. Only music soothes my soul in the same way. Perhaps that's because nature's orchestra is perfectly conducted by a knowing maestro.

I am inexplicably drawn, at times like this, to look inside myself for some of the answers that intrigue and challenge me to what this life is all about. This brief interval of freedom allows nature's open spaces to replenish the lack of space that we often feel inside. We all have our place of worship in some way, in some place or at some time. This just happens to be mine.

As I sit beneath the beacon I am fascinated by the competitive activity going on beyond this magnificent vista and marvel at how the inspiration of nature contradicts everything negative. It's a Shangri-La that abounds with positive energy.

The fishermen are casting relentlessly to find the right spot, changing tackle and position in the persistent pursuit of a strike. The yachtsmen are on their journey seaward for a day of recreational racing, sails trimmed to challenge the weather so they can be the best on the day. The kayakers are out in force targeting new time trials, pushing their limits, and the surfers are patiently pursuing the perfect wave. Everyone it seems is inspired to stretch their limits a little.

But it is the walkers and joggers who fascinate me the most. As I observe them walking the beach and heading for the beacon I notice that everyone *touches* the landmark. They then retrace their steps, obviously having achieved their halfway target. But everyone *touches* it. It's intriguing to observe that each runner has a goal to hit their target; to cross the imaginary line of personal attainment. It is a landmark everyone can see. And a target you can see is always the easiest to hit.

I am privileged to watch this recreational achievement. It confirms my belief that achievement is instinctive human behaviour. The spirit to win exists in us all, regardless of whether we are a participant or a spectator.

There's an old business proverb: 'Success belongs to those who act upon what they learn.' My challenge is for you to act on what you take from this text – not to necessarily emulate me, because what has worked for me may not apply to you, but to do what's real to you. To set your goals, and achieve them. Believe that they are attainable. There is no belief like true belief. Understand that there is a connection process from start to end and that all the pieces will fit. It's just finding the process that works for you and having the determination to go for it!

For me, my connection process was *The Bullseye Principle,* a simple business philosophy of self-improvement; being *good*, getting *better* to get the *best* result. It's beginning with a *good* idea, a worthwhile goal, then making the process in between *better* and giving it my *best* until I achieve my goal.

So try it. Use it to achieve *your* goals and hit *your* targets because it is very *do-a-bull*.

ACTION-A-BULL

Do you remember that old Aussie hit song 'I've been everywhere' by Lucky Starr? That lyric certainly applies to me. My speaking schedule takes me everywhere, and to places where I meet some wonderful people.

It was late autumn 2005. I was waiting for a flight at the Brisbane airport when a lady sitting in the lounge opposite approached me and remarked that she had heard me speak at a business conference in Fiji. Sharon Dawe was returning home to Young, a small country town in New South Wales almost two hundred kilometres west of Canberra. As we chatted, she told me that she owned a hair dressing salon in the town and boldly asked if I would consider coming to Young to speak to the local business community. Her persuasive reasoning was that for her business to be successful in a provincial town, the whole business community needed united performance standards.

So I readily accepted (enduring stopovers in Sydney and Canberra and a two hour car journey into a climate that plummets to zero degrees in winter) and two months later, I finally arrived in Young. It was worth the journey. Country people are so heart-warming and I gained as much from their wonderful reception as I hoped they gained from my business presentation.

What impressed me was a hundred people turned out at the local golf club on a frosty Sunday morning to hear me, and some had travelled from Canberra and Albury!

The event was a success, however, because Sharon had an idea when she saw me at the airport that would benefit her business colleagues. She then turned a good idea into action. Is it any wonder that 'Sharron's Hairline' is an award-winning business?

Good ... Better ... BEST!

Thomas Edison, whose ideas changed the world, once said: 'The value of an idea lies in the using of it.' His idea gave the world energy through the magic of electricity.

The most important energy is within us all. The spark of life is there for us all. Energy is what sets great businesses apart from their competition. But it is the spark that ignites that energy that is the real presence of the business. I can't emphasise enough how critical it is for one person to stand up and get the 'show on the road'. If you don't have a spark plug you can have a bunch of people sitting around agreeing about a great idea. Unless someone makes it happen, most of the time it doesn't. Are you the spark in your business?

The hardest thing when I started my business was to decide to get started.

I've heard it said many times, that the most common element among successful entrepreneurs is that they were at the right place at the right time and they took *action*.

> *Good ideas are common, the people who implement them are rare.*
>
> Michael Levine

BELIEVE-A-BULL

To get the best value from this book will depend on how committed you are to creating change and making progress in your life. We have one life and that's all; one chance to make our life everything that we would wish it to be. Some choose to let life dictate its harsh realities and accept the outcomes while others choose to control their destiny, realising that their destiny controls the future of others around them, particularly their family.

Think about it – the choice is yours. We become what we think about, because what we think about we *believe*.

My belief is that my *Bullisms* will stimulate *good* ideas that will assist you to prosper to a *better* level. To get the *best* result, however, refer to the illustration at the end of the chapter. You will see an empty Bullseye target. This is yours. Take a moment before you close the cover and think about a goal that you really want to achieve and that you believe you *can*. The moment we believe we can be whatever we want to be is the moment we discover our true potential.

Write your goal in the centre of the Bullseye. This is my connection process to you because I know if you write that goal *now,* then *The Bullseye Principle* won't end when you turn the final page. This will only be the end of the beginning for you. Success and happiness, however, are what you can end up with if you are willing to dream a dream, turn it into a goal and pursue that goal with every talent at your disposal.

BULLET POINTS

- The value of an idea lies in the using of it.

- Success belongs to those who act upon what they learn.

- The hardest thing when I started my business was to decide to get started.

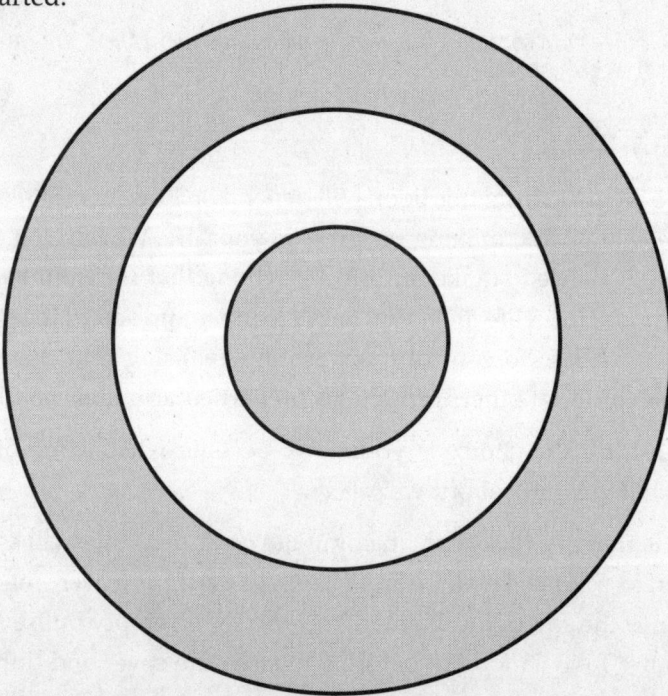

Chapter 22

A sentimental journey

BULLISM™: MEMOR-A-BULL

Time is the lens in which dreams are captured.

Francis Ford Coppola

Not so long ago, I was engaged to speak at a conference not far from where I grew up at Indooroopilly. I decided to visit the family home while I was in the district; a nostalgic trip to be sure, as the old house was sold years before, after my folks passed away.

My dad's old pub, where I first met Old Blue is now a thriving tavern, and the RSL hall is lost in a metropolis of urban development. It's moments like this I realise that the world I grew up in no longer exists. As I turned into Russell Terrace, I passed Moore Park and then, around the bend and up the hill, I saw the old house. It had changed, but somehow to me it looked just the same. I know that this sounds awfully like the lyric to Tom Jones's anthem, 'The Green Green Grass of Home', but this is why that song became a classic. Its story has a personal meaning to most of us at some time and at some place.

As I spotted the window to the room where I learned to play the guitar to my Elvis forty-fives, a young boy appeared, riding a bicycle in the front yard. Memories came flooding back of *my* childhood, and a lump swelled in my throat when I recalled the lessons learned from falling off *my* bike.

While the wallabies have long gone, I marvelled at how the familiar chorus of the 'maggies' and the currawongs blended harmoniously with the rhythm of the heavy traffic on the nearby Western Freeway.

On the seat beside me was my briefcase which contained the finished manuscript of this book. I was about to send it to my publisher. I couldn't help thinking about Old Blue who'd sowed the seed for this text fifty years ago. I wondered what he would have thought about all of this now. Life really is an amazing journey.

Success, I reasoned, is not a preordained thing. It's a constant balance between dealing with disappointment and recognising opportunity.

I was filled with emotion as I drove away from the place that contained my earliest memories. Passing Moore Park I had nostalgic recollections of grassboarding down its hilly slopes, kicking a football, skinny dipping in the creek and throwing homemade boomerangs. Life is like an unfailing boomerang. What you throw out goes full circle. It's the integrity in the throw, however, that determines the quality of the journey and the accuracy of the return. The nirvana of recently found success only mists over the essential journey.

Appendices

MEMOR-A-BULL MOMENTS

As you can tell, music has been my lifelong passion and I have been extremely fortunate to have selected a career that has been fulfilling to say the least. Therefore it is fitting to finish with a tribute to the entertainers I have had the opportunity to personally work with during my long-playing career. It humbles me to think that I have had the privilege to support their outstanding talent in some small way. Each one represents my most memor-a-bull musical moments.

My CBS years
– 1969–81

Air Supply

The Angels

Beach Boys

Chuck Berry

Johnny Cash

Cheap Trick

Chicago

Neil Diamond

Dragon

Bob Dylan

David Essex

Stephan Grapelli

Janis Ian

Billy Joel

KC and the Sunshine Band

Johnny Mathis

Meatloaf

Men at Work

Misex

Willie Nelson

Lou Rawls

Ivan Rebroff

Redgum

Marty Robbins

Santana

Boz Scaggs

Jeff Wayne (War of the Worlds)

Andy Williams

John Williams

My Toombul years 1981–2005

Tina Arena
Atomic Kitten
Bardot
Jimmy Barnes
George Benson
James Blundell
Daryl Braithwaite
Adam Brand
Bucks Fizz
Troy Casser-Daley
Nathan Cavaleri
Kate Ceberano
Kasey Chambers
Cockroaches
Harry Connick Jr
The Corrs
Michael Crawford
Shanley Del
John Denver
Slim Dusty
Tommy Emmanuel
Eurogliders
John Farnham
DJ Fontana
(Elvis's original drummer)
Foster and Allen
Simon Gallaher
Goo Goo Dolls
Adam Harvey
Marcia Hines
Hot Chocolate
Human Nature
Chris Isaak
Gina Jeffreys
Kamahl
Ronan Keating
Lee Kernaghan
Tania Kernaghan
Anne Kirkpatrick
Johnny Mathis
Reba Mcentire
Mental as Anything
Sophie Monk
James Morrison
Olivia Newton-John
Shannon Noll
Random
Rick Price
Charlie Pride
Cliff Richard
Leanne Rimes
Saddle Club
Melinda Schneider
Guy Sebastion
The Seekers
Karen Shaupp
Gene Simmons (Kiss)
Sister 2 Sister
Slayer
Ten Tenors
Pam Tillis
The Village People
Nikki Webster
The Wiggles
John Williamson

Index

Carey, Mariah 144
Carnegie, Andrew 86
Cash, Johnny 265
Casser-Daley, Troy 266
Cavaleri, Nathan 266
CBS Records 8, 12, 13, 19, 20, 126, 132, 134, 136, 137, 143, 144, 265
CDs 54, 70, 72, 73, 76, 91, 99, 100, 116, 117, 120, 121, 131, 162, 167, 173, 174, 176, 177, 232, 235, 254, 255
  illegal downloads 71, 173, 176
Ceberano, Kate 266
Centro Properties 195
Chambers, Kasey 266
Cheap Trick 265
Cher 179
Chicago 265
Churchill, Winston 26, 36, 122, 178
Cleghorn family 20
Clinton, Bill 53
Clooney, Rosemary 16
Coca-Cola 37, 90, 91, 167, 168, 182
Cockroaches 266
Coke, see Coca-Cola
Collins, Jim 183
Collis, Jack 212, 214
Commonwealth Centenary Medal 8, 13, 99
Como, Perry 16
Connick Jr, Harry 13, 102, 266
Cornwell, Allan 5
Corrs, The 9, 13, 54, 98, 102, 115, 266
Counts, The 8
Covington, Julie 137
Crate and Barrel 88
Crawford, Michael, 9, 98, 102, 131, 146, 147, 148, 266
Cruise, Tom 108, 136, 137
Curry-Kenny, Lisa 108, 109

D
Daimaru Department Store 194
Decca Records 238
Del, Shanley 266
Denver, John 9, 13, 98, 161–3, 165, 233, 266
Diamond, Neil 12, 19, 134, 143, 162, 179, 246, 265
Dion, Celine 144
Disney, Walt 32, 90, 92, 152, 217
Disraeli, Benjamin 27
downloads 71, 173, 176
Dragon 12, 265
Drucker, Peter 41
Dusty, Slim 9, 246, 248–52, 266
DVDs 54, 72, 73, 76, 92, 119, 157, 177
Dylan, Bob 265
Dyson, Brian 37, 182

E
Eagles, The 120, 179
Edison, Thomas 228, 259
Electrolux 91
Electronic Interiors 91–2
ELO 143
EMI 230, 234, 235, 238, 248
Emmanuel, Tommy 102, 163, 252, 255, 266
Essex, David 136, 137, 265
Eurogliders 266

F
Fact files 34, 50, 64, 70, 113, 170, 190, 205, 207, 215, 216, 217, 218, 223, 225
Farnham, John 102, 120, 179, 180, 240, 246, 266
Fizz, Bucks 266
Flight Centre, The 152
Fontana, DJ 266
Foster and Allen 266
Franklins Supermarkets 194
Friend, Bev 5